Caro & Co

Helping kids find

wonder

in the everyday

SALLY MILNER
PUBLISHING

First published in 2016 by
Sally Milner Publishing Pty Ltd
734 Woodville Road
Binda NSW 2583 AUSTRALIA

© Caroline Webster 2016

National Library of Australia Cataloguing-in-Publication data:

Creator: Webster, Caroline, author.

Title: Caro & Co helping kids find wonder in the everyday : easy outdoor and indoor activities to inspire kids of all ages / Caroline Webster.

ISBN: 9781863514972 (paperback)

Notes: Includes bibliographical references and index.
  Subjects: Caro & Co.
  Games.
  Play.
  Outdoor recreation for children.

Dewey Number: 790.1922

Design: Natalie Bowra
Printed in China

CAROLINE WEBSTER

Caro & Co
Helping kids find
wonder
in the everyday

easy outdoor and indoor activities to inspire kids of all ages

SALLYMILNER
PUBLISHING

Foreword

I was thrilled to be asked to write a foreword for this book.

Feeling awe and excitement about the natural world and environment around us is not a given. Generating this wide-eyed appreciation in children is a task and responsibility that not all parents, teachers and carers can do naturally. However, if we're given clues, tricks and techniques, opportunities to see and share awe can be grown in everyone. Inspiration is an addictive thing when it comes to seeing the world for what it can be. And this is exactly what "Helping Kids Find Wonder in the Everyday" set out to do and has achieved.

It's a book about bringing unstructured to the structured. Returning to the child scale and perspective. Putting on your ghost goggles, your wings of wonder, your shields of steel, your webs of wild, being unruly.

It's about turning back the time to the now. It's not about finding the past, it's actually about seeing the present without all the present day-to-day baggage and roles, labels and responsibilities that remove the magic, taint the time travel, lasso the lift-off and block the bravado of innocence.

This book is not so much about instruction as it is immersion and to immerse we have to let go. Letting go is liberation and freedom from a known quantity. Not every one of the activities in this book has a key learning outcome (KLO). The outcome is itself in the very activity. So in effect this book is actually for adults and the bonus is that you will help grow the very skills of perception, outlook and creativity in your children by not thinking about the end results but rather by letting them mature and blossom at the time that nature intends them to.

Explore, discover, retreat, observe, impart, imagination, compassion and sharing. These are just a few of the words that ooze from the pages.

This book is all about the educational abundance found in the simplicity of the everyday world around us. Lying on your back on the grass with your children is the equivalent of creating your own educational Cape Canaveral to launch understanding and inspiration. But not on a Space Shuttle budget! Nature doesn't set a budget – everything is free and abundant. What can I say about the exploration, discovery and cyclonic bliss of displacing a dandelion seed-pod to the four winds ~ nothing more than the description found on page 6.

This book is about fun. It is about games, shifting perspective but most importantly giving air to the educational opportunities that surround us in the everyday.

Letting go is in many ways the mantra behind this most valuable childhood resource. It's very rare to find such a valuable educational smorgasbord offering age-based structure within a framework of spontaneity and freedom. For any parent or educator, Nanna or Pop, Aunt or Uncle, this is a must have in your school bag of life.

Think of it as a handy workbook to return to over time to spark and jolt fresh views on how to create the magic and excitement that our children yearn to share and explore with us.

I hope you enjoy reading Caro's wonderful book as much as I have.

Costa Georgiadis
– Presenter, ABC's Gardening Australia

Contents

Acknowledgements

Books such as this, whilst an absolute pleasure to research and write, are never a solo effort. Many people have contributed to its creation and I'm grateful for their encouragement, tips and ideas.

I'd like to thank my children Angus and Grace for their patience and understanding as I disappeared into my office for days on end. Our experiences together, both indoors and outdoors, have shaped this book and for that I'm very grateful. They continually inspire me, and help me find wonder in everything we do.

My wish for them is that they continue to find amazement in the everyday and, when the time comes, motivate their own children to do the same.

To my wonderful husband Robert for his patience and love and for being official taste-tester for many of the recipes. Not a hard task for such a lover of food!

To Costa Georgiados for so readily agreeing to write a foreword for this book. Thanks to the inspirational Richard Louv for providing such a lovely endorsement of the book

My everlasting thanks to good friends from around the world, Bethe Almeras, Liz Ashton, Lis Chambers, Libby-Jane Charleston, Trish Duncan, Marghanita Hughes, Suz Lipman, Jo Nagle, Michelle Newton, Natasha Papworth, Reika Roberts, Susan Stewart, Amanda Watson and Karen Wilde for readily contributing recipes, advice, activities and support. They are all so very talented!

To Jenny Kable, an inspirational Early Childhood Educator, who readily provided such sound advice at the beginning of the book.

To my great mate Katrina Crook for supplying some beautiful images and her creative eye and ace advice on design.

To Libby and Ian at Sally Milner Publishing for believing in the importance of a book of this kind and for their guidance and expertise. Thanks too to Kathryn Lamberton who wasn't too vicious with her red pen and Natalie Bowra, a brilliant and intuitive designer.

And finally, to my beautiful mother Margaret for kick-starting my belief in and passion for all things magical and wondrous.

Introduction

When I was little, my mother gave me a birthday card. Apart from the standard birthday greeting, she wrote,

As you grow up, my wish for you is that you remember to use your words, love deeply and always strive to find wonder in the world around you.

It was such great advice and something I've attempted to do every day since.

Over the years I've asked over 500 people to name the one moment in their lives that filled them with wonder. Over 90% have responded with a memory of a special time spent outside; most often when they felt they were alone and discovering something extraordinary by themselves. Finding wonder has always been easy for me. It can be found everywhere, in the simplest of places and in many of the activities we undertake every day — you just need to know how and where to look. And, of course, wonder is amplified tenfold when you head outdoors.

Indeed, *'Go outside and find something to do'* was a common refrain in my home when I was growing up. Each time I stepped outside, the outdoors quickly became a mix of the magical and the practical.

A densely leaved shrub was a hideout from monsters, our dogs and, every now and then, Mum. A large tree was a home away from home. Everything was dragged up there including the dog and an entire tea set. It was also where we went when we got cranky and decided to run away from home. The vacant lot a couple of blocks away was where magical creatures lived and where my sisters, brothers and I often set off on dragon-hunting adventures.

The muddy laneway beside our home was the ideal place for baking mud pies and jumping in puddles. We had the perfect lavender bush where fairies dwelled — and where I experienced my first bee sting. We became little explorers and collected an extraordinary array of objects, some of which I still have today.

With no structured play, we unwound, recharged and spent plenty of time sitting still and watching nature do its thing. Being outside also taught us many lessons about the environment and our place within it. We learnt not to fear the outdoors, but to respect and love it. We also took the advice of our parents not to eat a berry without first checking with them and never to trust shiny black spiders.

We fought with free-range bantam hens for a patch of clean grass and still they rewarded us with delicious eggs each day. We tended our very small veggie patch with enthusiasm and love, the resultant vegetables, used to cook simple, delicious meals, made us wriggle with pride.

My own children are now teenagers and I regularly offer them the same advice I received all those years ago. Certainly, the advent of technology means I've had to work a little harder to help them remember to look for wonder around them in everything they do, and to actively engage with the outdoors and nature whenever they can.

Writing this book has been a joy. All the activities, either indoor or outside, are simple and inexpensive, and rely mostly on the ready imagination of your child. I might not be an educator but I am a mother who firmly believes that, if you are guided by your knowledge of your own child, together you can find a little wonder in everything you do. So go on. Open the door, step outside and find some magic.

What to expect

Remember, each child is an individual: unique and special in the way they explore and interpret the world around them. They have passions and fears that often only make sense to them. These will need to be handled, at times, with sensitivity and tolerance by those who love and care for them.

Children need time to play with others and by themselves. And they need interested adults who will encourage them as their skills and interests grow and who share their wonder and excitement outdoors. At times they will need you to temper their enthusiasm and keep a 'weather eye' out for safety issues relevant to their ability.

This outline is only a guide, with each age group building on the next. It is by no means definitive and you will know best how to manage your child's safety and wellbeing according to their skills and your own outdoor environment.

What your child will do outdoors

Two year olds

She is an accomplished indoors explorer who is seeing the world outdoors for the first time. She may be both fascinated and frightened.

Her skills are developing rapidly. She can walk up and down stairs, climb, kick and manoevre herself around on a tricycle.

She can express herself verbally, and use language to think, name items, communicate and influence others.

She will be interested in *doing* rather than *making* and will try and copy what you are doing in her play.

She will use simple tools like toy hammers and spanners, build with blocks and collect items of interest to *her*.

She will engage in sensory play as a way of learning about the world and throw herself (literally!) into what she is doing, with little appreciation for consequence. She is totally in the moment and absorbing experiences like a sponge.

The concept of sharing relates only to herself — what's mine is mine and what's yours is too. Help her to negotiate her turn or her share.

She may develop a 'passion' for something in the outdoors — it could be planes, trains, birds, insects, flowers.

She is irresistibly driven to repeat certain patterns in her play, such as gathering, transporting, and mixing items together.

She will love helping with the real tasks of the real world like cleaning, sweeping and gardening.

She will enjoy sharing simple songs and rhymes as part of her outdoor experience with you.

Three year olds

He will be developing more control over his body. His strength, agility, balance and coordination skills will all be improving.

He will run, jump, kick, throw with greater ability, but not always with greater accuracy.

He will engage in simple pretend play, often using you as his inspiration. This can be very scary!

He has an irresistible urge to throw things, gather things, climb, and hide in small spaces in his play.

He will want to do everything for himself and may become frustrated when his ideas don't work out. This may lead to spectacular temper tantrums and tears.

He will be learning to play alongside and with other children. He may be unsettled in mixed age groups and with siblings, due to his need to 'keep up' or assert his independence.

He is still developing an understanding of sharing toys and people.

His knowledge of simple concepts is growing and he may want to revisit games and experiences that he has enjoyed.

His interests and passions are growing and developing and he may surprise you with detailed knowledge about his chosen topic.

He may start to use songs and stories in his play. He thrives on feeling capable and responsible, and loves to help.

Four year olds

Her skills are increasing. She will be developing more accuracy and control when running, kicking, climbing, throwing, riding, jumping, etc.

She will be able to jump from a small height and climb ladders, small trees and steps with increasing ease, as well as turn corners and avoid things in her way.

She will engage in independent play for longer periods of time.

She will begin to understand that games often have rules, but will become confused and upset if the rules change.

She will start to devise her own experiments and make

Five year olds

His physical competence is developing and he is much better at looking after his own needs. He is more proficient at physical games, enjoys outings and may have progressed to a two-wheel bike.

He will concentrate for longer periods and engage in games with his peers that may extend for long periods, even days and weeks.

His pretend play will become more sophisticated and complex and he will begin to develop roles and themes.

He will want to spend time enjoying his own interests as well as playing with others.

His understanding of concepts and spatial relationships will increase.

He will now start to think before he acts or engages in outdoor play and to make decisions about what he wants to do or create.

Keen interests continue to develop.

Literacy and numeracy skills are developing and he will enjoy reading, DVDs, simple computer games and outings that support and build on these skills.

He will start to identify signs and notices while on outings and enjoy travel games and songs on family trips.

He may be ready for a short camping trip or outing with trusted friends and other family members.

decisions about what she wants. Making mud pies will take on a new meaning!

She will start to accept other children's ideas in play, while still having strong opinions about what she wants to do.

She is learning to spend time away from the family to engage with other people and her peers. She also needs to spend quiet time alone to watch and reflect.

She is learning to ask for help and will ask endless questions about her interests and yours.

She will express ideas and opinions based on her growing knowledge of the world. While humorous at times, it is very important to her that you take her seriously.

She will engage in make-believe play and often revisit or continue games over a period of days, and may even return to ideas weeks later.

This is the time of imaginary outings and friends.

Six year olds

She is continuing to build knowledge. She needs lots of time and opportunities to practise and perfect skills.

She will begin to differentiate between play and leisure and will enjoy both.

She will participate in group activities and develop greater understanding of outdoor games with rules.

Her physical activity levels will increase if she continues to have opportunities to participate in games and sporting activities relevant to her age.

She will be motivated by success and enjoyment.

She will need times for both active and quiet play.

Increasingly she will be able to take on responsibility for simple outdoor tasks at home.

If given the opportunity, she will start to develop hobbies and interests that relate to outdoor activities.

Times have changed but children haven't, and she will love to learn your old favourite games! What games did you enjoy outdoors as a child? Hopscotch? Skipping? What's the time Mr Wolf?

7–9 year olds

His strength and coordination improve rapidly during these years, and he begins to develop skills in more complex activities such as playing football and swimming.

He relishes a physical challenge, and will delight in practising and showing off new-found skills.

His play is complex and well organised, and he enjoys playing games with rules with small groups of friends, often of the same gender.

Although he enjoys forming friendships, and being a friend, at times he will still need adult support to negotiate the complex social world of the playground.

He is eager to please, and doing things the right way can become very important to him.

He is full of questions, voices his own opinions and engages in longer and more complex conversations.

He has a vivid imagination and still enjoys losing himself in the world of the imagination, which often involves complex plots and negotiating roles with friends.

His energy is boundless, and it may seem as if he never sits still.

His mental skills are now developing rapidly, and he learns best through active participation in hands-on activities.

He is more aware of the world around him and is developing a sense of conscience and right and wrong.

What you need to do outdoors

Two year olds

Let her spend time with you outdoors. This is an opportunity for her to build skills and learn about the world.

Look at your outdoor environment through the eyes of a sensory seeking two year old. If there are opportunities to play in sand, dirt and water, let her, but prepare for a mess!

Get down to her level and see the world from her point of view. This will help you anticipate her interests, as well as any safety issues before they become problems.

Be patient and tolerant of her need to explore.

Be there. She will have great plans and expectations that often outweigh her ability to implement them. She will need you around to help her achieve her dreams, to feel safe to explore, and sometimes to temper her enthusiasm.

Slow down. She will have her own play agenda and need time and space to explore her world in her own way.

Create rituals or routines. Two year olds thrive in a world that is familiar and predictable.

Involve her in everyday tasks: hanging out the washing, pulling weeds or watering the garden.

Plant some pots of colour and sweet smelling herbs. She will love helping you.

Give buckets, baskets and different containers to your two year old as she adores collecting and transporting things.

Provide opportunities for her to play with other children her own age as well as her siblings.

Follow and support her interests and let her begin to share yours. This builds connections, extends knowledge and creates relationships that will have lifelong benefits.

Take time to learn together and spend time playing with her. Model the skills you want her to learn.

Do let her have some private time for play. She doesn't need to know you are watching her every move!

Three year olds

You will need to assess safety issues and take precautions to accommodate his developing skills.

He will need simple and consistent behaviour limits that make sense to him.

Model safe and appropriate behaviour for your particular outdoor environment.

He still relies on the attentive presence of a nearby adult but not necessarily interacting or in the way.

He is intrigued by nooks and crannies and places to hide away from the prying eyes of adults. This may be as simple as hiding in a large cardboard box or sneaking behind a row of potted plants.

Provide simple toys and real props that can be used to extend his play. He will be drawn to balls, things that move, and things he can collect and carry about from place to place.

Create opportunities to help with adult activities using adult tools, especially if they combine a sensory element: digging in the garden, washing windows or washing the car.

Accept his interests, individuality and emerging personality.

Create opportunities to share your outdoor interests with your child but don't be disappointed if his interest is brief at this time. He will still enjoy being with you.

Spend some time as a family engaging in activities that you can all enjoy together.

Give him time to follow his own play urges and watch and wait as he discovers, invents and explores.

Four year olds

Effective supervision is important with your four year old. Allow more 'unsupervised' outdoor time at home – watch without her knowing you are there!

Create opportunities to play with others and widen her social circle. She may need your assistance to negotiate the terms of play, share ideas with others and take turns.

Monitor sibling rivalry. Set simple expectations and limits and be consistent in managing them.

Provide toys, resources and outings that will extend her developing skills. Bushwalking, swimming and trips to the park will offer different and increasing challenges and give her opportunities to practise her skills.

Give her increasing responsibility for chores at home. Remember, she may need reminders and good role modelling to complete them.

Accept that the standard she is capable of achieving may not be perfect, but is consistent with her ability at this time. Encourage her.

Enjoy her ability to make believe and pretend. Support her creativity and share her sense of wonder in make-believe.

Provide props so she can make her own imaginary world. She may enjoy building cubby spaces or making mud pies.

Start to share family stories about when you were little or when her grandma or grandpa was young. This creates connection and continuity and makes children feel safe and loved.

Build a library of reference books for young children about the natural world. She will enjoy finding out information about the creatures she encounters outdoors. Join in with your child's curiosity and wonder, and learn together!

Go for short family walks in natural spaces. Notice together what she is seeing, hearing and smelling. Encourage her to touch things in nature – to discover the smoothness of a rock or the rough texture of bark.

Embrace opportunities to play outdoors, whatever the weather. Be blown around in the wind, jump in rain puddles, stomp in the mud!

Five year olds

Provide increasing opportunities to play outside and build skills. Allow time for more complicated play and games and introduce family games in which he can participate.

Keep providing opportunities for him to spend time playing outdoors with friends.

Be on hand to help out when sibling rivalry or peer relationships get out of control. Make sure to establish and maintain clear limits and consequences to encourage appropriate behaviour.

Provide opportunities for risk and challenge in play within a framework of security and safety. Support him in assessing

his own risk and learning how to be safe and aware of others' safety.

Rejoice in his abilities and be tactful and supportive of skills that are still developing.

Help him to build resilience and persistence. Not everything worthwhile is easy. Model appropriate behaviours and responses to new challenges.

Leave time for him to sit under a tree and dream; time to unwind and de-stress is as important for him as it is for you.

Gather together an assortment of materials and objects to enrich your child's play. Ropes, pipes, lengths of wood, buckets, boxes and fabric are all examples of things that can be moved, changed, taken apart and used in a myriad of ways with no specific instructions.

Share your own delight in nature, and together explore the world of insects and creatures outside your door.

Encourage him to talk about the things he sees, hears, feels, smells and touches. It could be the sound of cicadas, the shape of the clouds or the taste of watermelon.

Six year olds

Recognise her strengths, interests and positive qualities, and let her know it is okay to try even if she makes mistakes.

Encourage resilience: help her learn to persist in worthwhile tasks by doing things together.

Model appropriate physical skills and behaviour.

Provide opportunities to develop responsibility.

Create time for free, independent play with friends. Enjoy planned outdoor experiences too.

Provide opportunities for group game participation. You can join in too!

Tailor her participation so that success is encouraged and her desire to continue participating is enhanced.

Ensure she has resources to encourage active participation. Balls, bats, Frisbees, skipping ropes, tyre swings, bikes etc. are all great.

Enjoy family picnics in the park, at the beach or even in your own backyard!

Support her in appreciating and caring for the natural environment. It could be caring for a worm farm, or helping her to plant and grow flowers, herbs, fruits and vegetables.

Support her hobbies and interests and share your own. Use technology as a tool to research what she is learning, but limit TV and computer time.

Above all, foster pleasure and enjoyment in the outdoors and you can't go wrong.

7–9 year olds

Negotiate ways to balance screen time with physical activity and outdoor play.

Begin your foray into organised sports or lessons, such as dance classes, swimming lessons and football.

Provide plenty of time for unstructured play amongst other activities such as homework and structured sports.

Share ideas and discuss important issues with your child. Engage him in conversations about the power and consequences of his actions and help him to see that his actions can effect change.

Role-model an active outdoor lifestyle by being active in your own life to show him that it is important and fun.

Give him responsibility for caring for or nurturing the natural environment around your home. It could be feeding a pet, weeding the vegetable patch, watering the garden or sweeping up leaves.

Increasing independence, confidence and physical ability make this an important time to discuss water safety and road safety with your child.

Jenny Kable, Early Childhood Educator and blogger - Let the Children Play

Let's get going

Outdoors means different things to different children. Depending on where you live, it could mean a small apartment balcony, a suburban backyard, a rural property, the corner park or playground, the beach, the bush, or a mix of all these. All will interest a young child and each has its own unique lessons to impart.

When you do decide to head outside, remember that children need time to explore and discover — by themselves and at their own speed. Ditch as much structure as you can and be guided by your child's imagination. Encourage a balance of messy rough and tumble, quiet times of reflection and learning, and a good dose of make-believe.

Be prepared to regularly retreat, to let your child discover and explore on their own. It is my view that unstructured play is one of the greatest gifts we can give our children.

Just like every other experience in their lives, children will love the outdoors one day and hate it the next. They may want to turn the entire garden over to vegetables in one hour and then lose interest completely. Be prepared to have several goes at things. However, as children get older they will generally be more willing to stay outside for extended periods of time, and they will become more adept at finding or creating adventure on their own.

Sometimes neither of you will feel like going outside. Remember, you can choose when you and your child go outdoors; you don't need to be outdoor warriors, nor should you feel guilty about turning on the television instead of going for a walk together. Rather, consider the outdoors as a ready resource that you can add to the everyday mix of your lives — at a pace, time and style to suit you both.

Here is a list of things you might like to have on hand before venturing outdoors, followed by some important safety issues.

Equipment outdoors:

- sunscreen
- hat
- water
- wipes or tissues
- Band-Aids®/Elastoplast
- insect repellent
- camera
- notebook or journal

The following is a list of things I have collected, made or purchased over a period of time, which you may find useful to have stored away somewhere:

- simple children's gardening kit
- bug-catcher (see page 118)
- journal (any large sketch or notebook will do)
- empty fisherman's tackle box for storing all those priceless found objects
- box of simple bits and pieces (such as string, pieces of wood of irregular shape and size, sticky tape, rubber bands, pieces of cardboard, wooden boxes, shoe boxes, buttons, stickers, child-safe glue, old containers and jars, paint brushes, non-toxic paints, paper bags, glitter, pipe cleaners)
- potting mix and some face masks
- bag of straw
- magnifying glass
- empty Nespresso™ pots

Safety

A child's safety outdoors is paramount. However, it shouldn't stop you from sharing as much time as you can outside with your child. Commonsense and knowledge of your child and their abilities will, as much as possible, ensure a safe environment.

From the very beginning, establish clear and non-negotiable safety limits and boundaries that work for your household. Limits will differ. For example, you might decide that:

Your child is not allowed to handle garden tools until she has a good understanding of the associated safety issues.

You and your child must always hold hands while crossing the road.

Opening the front gate/door is not allowed unless you are present.

As they get older and venture out without you, they must always have at least one friend with them at all times.

I am not a safety expert, but the following are what I consider some essential and commonsense rules:

- Be present with your child in the outdoors at all times (or be able to see what they are doing) until you are comfortable that they can spend time alone outside.

- Supply hats, sunscreen and plenty of water when your children play outdoors.

- Give your child individual attention when you can.

- Be aware of any external factors that may cause allergic reactions in your child (for example, pollen, bee or wasp stings, some plants, sap and grasses, chlorine, pets).

- Give simple and positive safety reminders.

- Practise good hygiene.

- If flying kites or other airborne objects, look up first for power lines.

Chemicals and tools

Instil early in your child a healthy respect for any chemicals that might be found in your immediate environment, including pool and gardening chemicals. Ensure these are stored in a secure place, out of reach of young children. As children get older and their curiosity and independence develop, chemicals can be fascinating, but remind them that these continue to be a potential risk.

When not in use, keep gardening tools stored safely out of reach of tiny hands. When you are playing or working in the garden together, ensure that tools are not left lying about to be tripped over or in easy reach of toddlers.

Flora and fauna

Imparting a love of plants and an early understanding of the critical role they play in sustaining life on earth is easy. The sheer diversity and beauty of plants enthral children and tell their own story. However, it is important to explain early the need to be aware of the potential toxicity of plants.

Please don't let this panic you, but do seek ongoing advice from plant specialists at a nursery as to which are poisonous and unsuitable for home gardens. The knowledgeable staff at your local botanic gardens are also a great resource as too are gardening magazines and the internet.

If children are bitten or stung, determine immediately what has caused the injury and seek appropriate medical attention.

On an average day outside, children will come across an amazing number of creatures — mostly without knowing it. Again, lessons taught early about those animals or insects that pose poisoning risks are critical. Be positive when talking about fauna as children can be easily scared and develop an ongoing and unnecessary fear.

Included in these safety talks should be an introduction to the innate behaviour and needs of family pets.

Scale for recipes in the following activities

How hard is it? This is a number out of five that reflects the difficulty of the recipe. One is the lowest in difficulty and five is the highest.

Will it be messy? A number out of five that reflects the level of mess you can expect the recipe to generate. One is the least mess and five is the most.

Is there much to do? A general idea of how long the recipe will take to prepare.

How many or how much? This gives a general idea of how many people a recipe will feed or how many serves it will make.

Age level? A guide to the age of the child the recipes are best suited to. Be guided by your own child's abilities because every child has different capabilities.

Nature's Wonders

Wondering

Finding

wondering

The outdoors is where imagination and discovery collide in the most spectacular fashion. Mother Nature's secrets are just begging to be discovered and, what's more, she is a brilliant, patient teacher and your child a willing student. Everything outdoors is full of wonder.

A couple of feathers stuck in their hair and your child is instantly Geronimo or Pocahontas. Long clusters of berries make beautiful earrings, an agapanthus stem turns into the ultimate sword and a cicada skin creates the perfect brooch. Nearly every object found outside can become something special as Mother Nature offers the most fantastic props box from which to draw.

Encourage your child to find the extraordinary in the ordinary, the magic in the mundane and enchantment in the everyday. Here are some ideas on how to go about this.

Whizzing clouds

On a warm lazy day, we like nothing better than heading outside, lying on the grass and watching the clouds go by. Every shape and object is up there, and watching and describing them can encourage stillness, independent thought and imagination. Older children can be encouraged to name the cloud types – cirrus, cumulus, nimbus, and so on. They might even want to do some further research when you head home.

Just the other day my son saw a perfect heart scudding across the sky, so I encourage you to head outdoors when you can and see what you and your child can find.

Fairy rescue

Set the scene for young children by suggesting that you have seen a few sad fairies lurking around the garden. Perhaps a bird stole their home? Or a nasty lizard blundered through it, leaving it in tatters? Or, horror of horrors, Dad may have mown over it last weekend! Encourage them to build a new home and place it in a quiet spot in the garden.

Your children can find all the necessary equipment themselves, with you offering a suggestion on decor every now and then, or when invited.

In the past, my children have used moss, lichen, dandelion-seed clusters, dainty flowers and cut grass to great effect. Occasionally, they have chosen items from inside, such as bread, dog biscuits, sultanas, grape tomatoes and bits of carrot.

This is a wonderful way for children of all ages to spend an afternoon – and it encourages imagination, compassion and sharing.

nature's wonders

Dastardly dandelions

Another simple game of make-believe is to encourage children to pick and blow dandelion-seed clusters into the air.

With just a little prompting, children will quickly come to know that they are really releasing a million trapped fairies from the evil clutches of the dastardly dandelion and will be granted a wish in return. My daughter, now 13, still delights in playing this game.

High Tea

Take a visit to the two-dollar shop and buy a child's tea set, or head to the local charity store and purchase some old-fashioned teacups and saucers. Present them to your children with an old tablecloth, some paper serviettes and water in a drink bottle (or squeezy dispenser for young children). Or you can simply encourage them to run to and from the garden tap, filling their cups.

Their imaginations are likely to run wild from here, or you might like to set the scene for them — you could suggest that they invite the Queen of the Fairies or the King of the Trolls (who can be very polite if asked nicely) for high tea. Fairies, of course, don't eat human food, so your children will need to collect what they believe is appropriate fare. Now retreat and let their imaginations take hold. If you don't receive an invitation to the party, celebrate your children's independence.

Weather watching

Experiencing the weather in all its forms can be fun! From windy days, when everything seems to hang on for dear life, to impossibly hot and sunny days, or wild storms that encourage you to batten down the hatches and sit at the window watching, there's something for everyone (see 'Storm watch' on page 25).

There's still huge excitement in our home when a rainbow splashes across the sky. Little children will love counting and naming the colours and then setting off to get to the end of it. Older children can be encouraged to think about why rainbows form and which atmospheric conditions need to occur before they can. And, of course, everyone should be encouraged to draw or make their own version of a rainbow after returning from trying to find that elusive pot of gold.

Windy days are also magic. Flying a kite is fun. Or head to a park and encourage your children to imagine themselves as leaves being blown about. Join in with them as they run, yell and roll about, trying to catch the wind. Take some bubble blowers for the full effect – it's exhilarating!

sparkly shadows

Reflected light fascinates children. My daughter still loves taking a reflective object (sparkly necklace, tin foil or a small mirror) outdoors on a sunny day and finding a spot where she can make it reflect a myriad of tiny rainbows or prisms onto a wall or the ground. She also infuriates our dog by reflecting the light onto the floor and laughing madly as he tries to catch it with his paws. Older children can be encouraged to consider how sunlight can be refracted and why it reflects the way it does.

On the whole, children are also fascinated by the amazing array of shadows cast by both our natural and built environments. They love creating shadow puppets (using their body or whatever else is to hand), from the simple bunny (clenched fist with two fingers protruding) through to amazing critters limited only by their imagination.

nature's wonders

Rainbow sandwich

DIFFICULTY **1** MESS FACTOR **2** PREP TIME **5 MINS** COOKING TIME **N/A** FEEDS **2**

4 slices of soft, awesomely fresh, preservative-free white bread

1 large carrot, grated

1 large stick of celery, sliced thinly

1 Lebanese cucumber, washed, thinly sliced

Half a raw beetroot, peeled and grated

Raspberry jam

Peanut butter

A few lettuce leaves, washed and roughly torn

Your child can help with nearly every aspect of this delightful sandwich packed with colour, texture and taste. I'm yet to find a child who won't wolf it down in two or three bites.

Method

Spread two pieces of bread with a layer of peanut butter. Spread the other two with a layer of raspberry jam. Sprinkle all the other ingredients evenly on top of these layers. Squish the slices of bread together, cut into four and enjoy.

If your child is nut intolerant, forego the peanut butter, or replace it with a little bit of tahini. Or if you don't want to make a sandwich, consider a rainbow salad!

Make-believe houses

Children enjoy creating rooms, or even a whole house, if they have a little space outdoors. This can be as simple as stepping out an imaginary floor plan and then outlining it with sticks or long leaves. They then choose their favourite room and collect things to decorate it, perhaps their pillow and a blanket for a bedroom or several saucepans, cups and a few bits of cutlery for a kitchen.

Shops are also big favourites. Everything in the outdoors can be sold, and gumnuts or other funky seedpods can be used for currency! Relying only on their beautiful imaginations, this is a great way to spend an afternoon.

Potions 101

If you have a budding Harry Potter or Hermione Granger in the family, magical potions will be concocted at some stage. With nothing more than a container or two, some water and whatever is within reach, children can dream up some truly awesome (and awful) potions. Think soil, dog biscuits, washing up liquid, leaves, flowers, sultanas, food dye.

Children delight in selecting the ingredients and pouring them from container to container. Even if your child has never heard of Harry Potter, this sensory, unstructured play, with its mix of touching, pouring, collecting, earthy smells and murky colours, thrills young children.

If you have access to some soft stone (sandstone, chalk, limestone, etc.), your older children may like to spend some time pounding, grinding and smashing it to produce perfect fairy or dragon dust to add to their potion.

Junior DETECTIVES

Kids are natural explorers. Whether they are dragon slayers on a mission to rescue the family pet (who you may subsequently find tied to the clothesline) or budding scientists on the trail of a magical creature is entirely up to them.

With little or no input from you, they are likely to create the most fantastic scenarios and a whole other world into which they will (for a period of time) fully immerse themselves.

Magical creatures might be elusive, but your children (with no need for costumes other than what they can find in the garden) will be certain of their existence and are likely to want to continue 'hunting for signs' again and again.

After bedtime, you could add to the set by placing some mysterious objects around the garden: large white pebbles (dragon poo), a few snapped branches or stomped-upon plants (proof of magical creatures), glitter (indicating elusive fairies) can all add to the theatre.

back-to-front day

A fun activity for kids of any age is to hold a back-to-front day. Simply muddle up a typical day by changing the order of things. It's sure to spark your child's imagination and promote discussion on why we do things the way we do. For example, you might like to start your day with dinner. Then have a bath but stay in your pyjamas. If you're brave enough, take the family pet for a walk in your PJs. Have breakfast for lunch and then lunch for dinner. It's bound to confuse everyone, but it's great fun and will fill your day with laughter.

Make-believe in the kitchen

Most kids love to get into the kitchen and it's important that they do, as they will learn some important life skills, not least of which is to begin understanding where foods actually come from. And kids love playing grown-ups, so I guarantee they will adore being given the opportunity to cook something for you.

Why not encourage your children to set up their own restaurant or outdoor café? Depending on their age, it can be an entirely imaginary meal, but the table can still be set, things can be cooked on an imaginary stovetop and culinary delights served. For older kids you might want to help them devise an age-specific menu and let them get on with it. They could cook a simple meal for the entire family. Some pan-fried sausages with mashed potatoes and greens on the side would be a great start. Encourage them to do some baking too. If they are a little unsure about baking a cake from scratch, there are some great packet cakes available nowadays which make the process much easier.

Grandma's simplicity chocolate cake

DIFFICULTY **1** MESS FACTOR **3** PREP TIME **15 MINS** COOKING TIME **25 MINS** FEEDS **6-10** DEPENDING ON SLICE THICKNESS

1 cup self-raising flour

2 heaped tbsp of cocoa powder

½ cup white sugar (raw sugar will intensify the flavour)

80 g butter

½ cup full-cream milk

2 eggs

A good friend shared this recipe with my daughter a couple of years ago. Aptly named because it is easy for children to master, it's now a regular in my daughter's baking armoury. It is a perfect cake for a kids' afternoon tea and is also a great addition to a picnic lunch. Your children will gobble this cake up in no time! Children under 5 can be your eager helpers; children 6+ can have a go at this recipe by themselves.

Method

Preheat your oven to 180°C. Put all the ingredients into a mixing bowl. Using a wooden spoon (there is no need to use a blender), stir until the ingredients are well combined. Transfer to a lightly greased cake tin and bake in the oven for 20 minutes or so. The cake doesn't really need icing; instead, sprinkle over some icing sugar and serve while still warm.

nature's wonders

finding

A young child's environment is both vast and intimate. For very young children, understanding the environment beyond their own little patch of outdoors, and the creatures that inhabit it, is impossible to grasp. However, as they develop, children will begin to see themselves as part of something bigger and will be eager to learn and discover more about the big wide world and themselves.

Below are lots of activities that will encourage your children to develop curiosity about the world around them.

Why does it do that?

Asking your child lots of questions about the outdoors can greatly assist their journey of discovery. For example, you might ask:

Why do you think we have plants?

Why are there so many different animals?

Why do you think we have soil?

Why do you think the sun is hot?

Why does the wind blow the way it does?

Why do you think we have fire/air/water?

Why do you think there are insects?

No answer is wrong, but certainly each one will help your child begin conceptualising the environment and their place in it.

The flow-on effect of these discussions is that children will also unknowingly absorb messages about independence, resilience and compassion. Older children might want to head to the computer to research these concepts in more detail.

Garden chaos

**This is a completely crazy activity to consider if you are trying to create order in your garden.
But you know what? It is so much fun for children of any age that I think the resulting chaos is well worth it.**

Together, visit your local garden centre and randomly choose six seed packets. Encourage your child to choose plants that appear to be completely different from one another in size, colour, structure and shape.

To avoid disappointment, try and make sure that at least a couple of the plants your child chooses will actually grow (that is, the plants are suited to the space and season you have chosen for this activity).

On the whole, nasturtiums, beans, sunflowers, pumpkins, zucchini, tomatoes, marigolds, violas (pansies), Cosmos, Gaura, parsley, chives, rocket, kale, rainbow chard and spinach are all good options.

Once at home, find a clear space in the garden. Open the seed packets, tip them into a bowl and mix with a little coarse sand if you have some to hand. Then, standing together with your back facing the garden bed, toss the seed mix over your shoulder. Rake over lightly and keep well watered for the first couple of weeks.

The result – who knows? Some weeks later, plants could spring up sporadically (or not at all), or you may get a wild profusion of seriously odd-looking plants competing for space all at once.

This activity encourages patience and will hopefully provide a visual and, in some cases, culinary delight for you and your children.

nature's wonders

Water, water everywhere

Water is one of the four basic elements of our world (if you believe ancient philosophers and astrologers). Certainly, along with air, fire and earth, water is essential to life.

Talking about different forms of water and explaining its role in sustaining life is not as difficult as you might think. Find a variety of simple containers, old PVC pipes, a hose and a watering can and you can create lakes, waterfalls, oceans (add a little salt), rivers, ponds, rain, puddles and even a beach (collect some sand and seaweed for the full effect). Encourage older children to find out what constitutes water, why it evaporates, where it goes, when and why we drink it and how plants use it.

Rain, rain, come any day!

Not only is this activity really good fun, but making a rain gauge can be a starting point for discussion about the need to conserve water. To make one, you will need:

- a large PET plastic bottle cut in half
- a few large, thick rubber bands
- a big sturdy straight stick
- a ruler
- a permanent marker.

Mark intervals in millimetres (or the measurement of your choice) on the side of the bottle or simply attach a ruler to the bottle with a rubber band. Then attach the bottle to the stick using more rubber bands. Insert the stick firmly into an open spot in your garden where nothing will overhang the gauge.

Help your child to devise a chart on which he can track rainfall over the year and remind him to check his rain gauge after rain. (He may well become quite the rain 'watcher' and run to the gauge whenever a shower has fallen.) Older children might like to create a more complicated perpetual calendar to chart not only when rain falls but also all types of atmospheric conditions.

storm watch...

Observing the weather is a good starting point for discussions on wind, air, clouds, and other atmospheric phenomena. In particular, thunderstorms provide the most amazing visual experiences for children: the changing colour of the sky, billowing clouds and lightning in its many forms make great theatre.

Safety is paramount when setting off to observe changeable weather, particularly when lightning is about. Some children (and the family pet) are terrified of thunderstorms, so be guided by your knowledge of your child to determine not only whether it's safe to head out, but how your child will react to the experience.

Go to a safe, protected spot for uninterrupted viewing. Driving to the beach and staying in your car can be a good option. Never shelter under a tree and always avoid open spaces. Pack a camera or journal and let your children snap or draw while they watch the display. Also encourage them to talk about where the weather comes from and why it is doing what it's doing.

You might like to check with your local weather bureau before undertaking this activity. As a general rule of thumb, if you count the seconds between thunder and lightning, and it is under 30 seconds, it most likely means that the storm is less than 10 km (6.2 miles) away and it is probably advisable to stay indoors.

nature's wonders

All creatures

All creatures deserve a place in the environment although, frankly, some can look quite frightening and easily scare children. It's important though, to reinforce that everything has its place and that we need animals and insects as much as they need us. For example, try to resist killing a simple house spider. Instead, remind your children that these spiders are the natural enemy of flies and mosquitoes.

Encouraging children to learn about the diversity of the animal kingdom and our interdependency has several benefits. It instils compassion, ignites the imagination and encourages respect for all creatures.

Watching small insects go about their everyday lives can mesmerise young children – the busier the insect, the quieter the child. Industrious little ants going around in circles, or marching proudly in a frenetic but seemingly straight line, will fascinate your child. A spider busying herself in a web, scuttling to and fro until the perfect shape is achieved can also have the same effect.

Do remember, when observing insects, that a bite or sting can be poisonous, so children should keep their distance until you are sure it's safe for them to handle them.

Canine capers

On a warm day, many children love getting wet and soapy with the family pet. If the weather permits, encourage your kids to get into their bathers and then soap your dog from head to toe, give him a good scrub and hose him clean in the back garden. Let the dog (and the children) tear around the yard for lots of fun while drying off. A game of fetch might be in order at this point, too.

Never leave your children alone with the dog during this activity, as it may be fearful of the water. This is also a good time to talk about the need for them to respect your dog and explain some of its innate behaviours. As a general rule, I would discourage ever leaving children alone with the family dog until they are at least 10 years of age.

nature's wonders

ANIMALIA

There are many creatures you might like to consider for your children when the time is right. Pet fish, hermit crabs and ant farms (see page 65) are all relatively easy for children to tend, yet still impart positive messages about responsibility and the various needs and habits of different animals. Consider silk worms if you have access to a mulberry tree. Moving upwards on the scale of care required, you might consider rabbits, hamsters, guinea pigs, mice, cats or birds.

And if you fancy a trip down memory lane, why not buy your child some sea monkeys? All the rage in the late 1960s and 70s, they are brilliant fun and still available via the internet today.

Speedy snails

While snails are the bane of most gardeners' lives (see page xx for suggestions on how you and your children can get rid of them), they can also be fun to play with before you move them along.

Place a hula hoop, or part of a garden hose looped to form a circle, in a shady spot with a flat surface, if possible. Ask your children to find a snail each. They might want your help with this, as little ones may not like touching them. Also, some people can have an allergic reaction to them. If this is the case, make sure your child wears gloves.

When each child has a snail, mark the shells with some coloured chalk or nail polish to make them easily identifiable (use a different colour for each snail). Place them in the centre of the circle and the race is on! The snail which gets to the edge of the circle first wins. The snails may spend some time hiding in their shells before they set off, but eventually their desire to escape will overcome them.

When Christmas beetles are about, you can race them as well, although they do have a tendency to fly away. And if you can cope with the thought of large cockroaches, they are also fun to race – they are the Speedy Gonzales of the insect racing fraternity! But forget ants, they just go around in circles.

Make sure everyone washes their hands after this activity.

nature's wonders

Wriggly Worms

Some children are very brave when it comes to handling these harmless but slippery little creatures. That's fantastic, but don't push it if they're genuinely fearful. When disturbed from their underground home, worms will wriggle like fury in your hand, which can be quite disconcerting.

You may notice that after a heavy shower of rain they appear lemming-like on your footpath or paving, intent on dying in the sun. What's really happening is their home has become flooded and they've fled looking for higher, drier ground. Sadly, most won't find their way home (unless you give them a hand) but they will make a tasty meal for a bird. This is great for the bird, but sad for you (and the worm!) because they are so very good for your garden, keeping the soil aerated with their little tunnels, while their poo (castings) provides a wonderful natural fertiliser for your plants.

Healthy soil is a fundamental component of a healthy planet, so I encourage you to help your child learn to love soil and respect these harmless, but beneficial, little wrigglers. Perhaps you could find an area of soft soil and let your younger children dig away, searching for them? Older children might want to have a go at building a worm farm (see page 52). (See also The Perfect Mud Pie on page 100, Super Sleuth on page 116, and Catch That Insect on page 118 for other activities using soil.)

nature's wonders

— a place to be Me

Overloaded with structured play, organised sport, the distraction of technology and the general busyness and cacophony of a household, young children can easily become worn out and occasionally stressed.

Taking time outside can be a natural antidote to children's busy lives. Without anyone telling them what to do or how to do it, the opportunity for private, quiet play or rest is a time for young minds and bodies to unwind and be at peace. And these periods of reflection can impart a sense of belonging and foster a connectedness with the world around them.

Encouraging private time in this way develops stillness, independence and resilience in your child. I once found my daughter fast asleep with a beautiful smile on her face, deep in the recesses of her secret hideaway.

On the whole, children adore having their own little private place outside where they can just sit and be, store treasures, or invite their friends for a game of their choosing. It might be under a low-hanging tree, in among the shrubs, or at the top of a small tree.

Encourage them to find their own secret hideaway and, in so doing, experience a good dose of magic, although it's also where the wild things are and where they themselves can be wild for a few hours. Whichever spot and activity they choose, celebrate their independence and knock three times before entering!

Let's go catch a bus!

Most children love a trip on public transport. Be it a bus, train, ferry or plane, it can offer a new and exciting experience for them. So, consider a trip together on a rarely used form of transport. It might be a ferry ride over the harbour or a train trip to the shops and back. My 14-year-old son still much prefers taking public transport when he can. I think it has something to do with his burgeoning independence as he is old enough now to travel by himself, but also because it offers so much 'colour and movement' and the perfect opportunity to silently observe strangers. I recall a ferry trip with my daughter when she was about two that had no purpose other than being on a ferry. We spent half the day just hopping on and off ferries, cruising around our harbour with the smell of the salt in our noses, watching other marine craft whiz by. It was such fun to share the experience with her and cost next to nothing. It is still her preferred mode of transport.

If your children are a bit older, before you travel encourage them to do a bit of research on their chosen mode of transport. For example, if they choose a tram, find out who invented them, in which countries they are used and why, and the fundamentals of how they operate. The internet provides endless information on public transport. Younger children might simply like to do some drawings of their favourite machine or take photos when you actually travel.

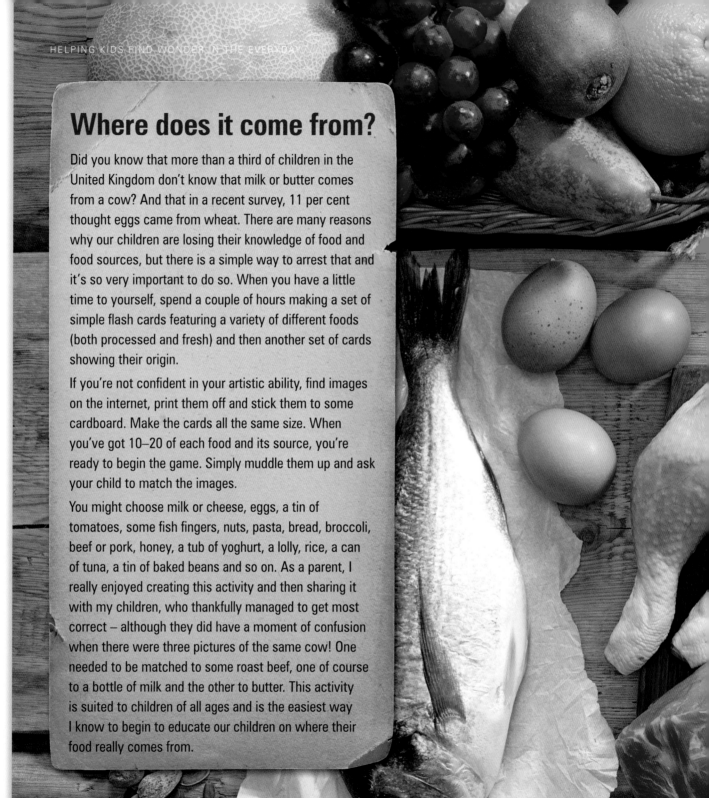

Where does it come from?

Did you know that more than a third of children in the United Kingdom don't know that milk or butter comes from a cow? And that in a recent survey, 11 per cent thought eggs came from wheat. There are many reasons why our children are losing their knowledge of food and food sources, but there is a simple way to arrest that and it's so very important to do so. When you have a little time to yourself, spend a couple of hours making a set of simple flash cards featuring a variety of different foods (both processed and fresh) and then another set of cards showing their origin.

If you're not confident in your artistic ability, find images on the internet, print them off and stick them to some cardboard. Make the cards all the same size. When you've got 10–20 of each food and its source, you're ready to begin the game. Simply muddle them up and ask your child to match the images.

You might choose milk or cheese, eggs, a tin of tomatoes, some fish fingers, nuts, pasta, bread, broccoli, beef or pork, honey, a tub of yoghurt, a lolly, rice, a can of tuna, a tin of baked beans and so on. As a parent, I really enjoyed creating this activity and then sharing it with my children, who thankfully managed to get most correct – although they did have a moment of confusion when there were three pictures of the same cow! One needed to be matched to some roast beef, one of course to a bottle of milk and the other to butter. This activity is suited to children of all ages and is the easiest way I know to begin to educate our children on where their food really comes from.

Chicken

nature's wonders

Making the most of each day

Outdoor
activities

Indoor
activities

outdoor activities

Every day outside is different. There are always chores to do (some more pleasant than others) and variations in weather can provide surprises along the way. Whether you are watering, weeding, camping, cycling, walking the dog or hanging out the washing, spending a little time with your child undertaking them together will not only help get the chores done, but you'll both have loads of fun along the way.

Let's do it!

Young children never seem to stop moving. Celebrate and encourage their enthusiasm (and stamina) with some fun outdoor endeavours.

All children require regular physical activity and fresh air to help their developing little bodies become the best they can be. Now I'm not recommending that you head out every day and groom your child to run a half-marathon before the age of six – that's just crazy. Instead, I suggest you try and develop a regular schedule of everyday activities that fits in with your lifestyle and gets you both out and about. It doesn't have to be constructed activity or play: a daily walk around the neighbourhood or simply kicking a ball together in the back yard is a great start.

You might also wish to consider taking some typically 'indoor' activities out. Drawing and colouring in, card games, constructing Lego®, reading books, playing handheld computer games, playing dress-ups or make-believe (such as shopping, cooking, cleaning) can all be done outside with little or no extra effort.

Walking and running

Sometimes the simplest outdoor activity can be the most satisfying. When you have time, consider a walk or small run. It may surprise you just how far your child's little legs can take them, while they chat happily about what they see, hear and smell.

And on a free day, consider heading to the hills for a bush walk. Pack a simple lunch, a compass, water, sunscreen, mobile phone and hats and enjoy everything that wide-open space has to offer. Always remember to let someone know where you are planning to go.

This is a wonderful way for children of all ages to spend an afternoon – and it encourages imagination, compassion and sharing.

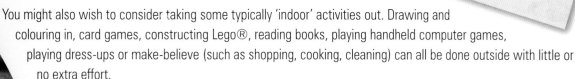

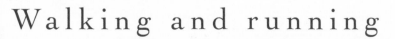

making the most of each day

Cycling

There's a bicycle to suit children in every age group. Cycling is not only great exercise; it encourages coordination and independence and is a starting point for road awareness.

If you have access to a bush track or semi-rural area, riding through muddy puddles can be a magical experience. Or why not consider hiring a tandem bike and going for a ride together? Many local councils have installed bike tracks in local parks for young children, complete with road signs and traffic signals.

Remember to pack a safety helmet, sunscreen and water and set limits about where, when and with whom your children ride their bikes.

cheesy damper

DIFFICULTY **2** MESS FACTOR **3** PREP TIME **15 MINS** COOKING TIME **30 MINS** FEEDS **4-6**

¾ cup grated tasty cheese (optional)

3 cups self-raising flour

Pinch of salt

Water

For a bit of extra flavour you could add onion, sweet corn kernels, gherkins, herbs … the list is endless.

Method

Mix the cheese, flour and salt with just enough water to form a firm dough. Shape into a flattened ball. The damper can be cooked in a billy, with the lid on, hung over your campfire. Or place the dough (wrapped in foil if you wish) in a hole you've dug and cover thickly with some hot coals and ashes from the fire. Leave to cook for about 30 minutes, then remove, dust off, slice and eat!

Row, row, row your boat

If you have access to the beach, a river, creek or lake or even a large dam, kayaking, canoeing or rowing is a great way to while away a sunny morning or afternoon.

Encourage your children to have a turn at the paddle/oars, trail their hands in the water, and look for the fish and other water creatures below.

Remember sunscreen, lifejacket, hat, water and a change of clothes – for both of you!

CAMPING

You know what? I love everything about being outside, but I just don't like camping. But my children, and thankfully their dad, adore it. They started in the back garden, but they have progressed to the point where they undertake all-out attacks on a national park once or twice a year.

They love the experience of getting really dirty for a few days, eating rustic meals (or three days' worth of sausage sandwiches), not having their mother around, boiling a billy, reciting bush poetry, telling scary stories, star gazing and snuggling up in a tent for the night.

If you have similar outdoor warriors in your family, camping is the perfect way to foster a love of the outdoors and give those who are less keen the opportunity to sleep in!

making the most of each day

THE
big blue

Once you think your children are old enough, spend a day snorkelling in the depths of some large rock pools at your local beach. You might need to spend a little time showing your child how to breathe correctly through the snorkel. (A lake or river is also a great alternative if you don't have ready access to the beach.) It's a whole other world down there and children will be mesmerised.

Before you set out, you might want to do a little research to find out which sea creatures are local to your area, so you can more easily identify them once you're in the water. When you return home, encourage your children to do some drawings of what they have seen. If a love of snorkelling persists, older children may well want to start saving their money towards a scuba diving course. The internationally recognised PADI course can be undertaken once your child turns 10.

making the most of each day

Going bush

I read somewhere recently that only a third of children under the age of 10 have visited a farm more than once. So if you have a friend or relative who owns a farm, try and wangle a visit every now and then. I can guarantee that children from the Big Smoke will find them magical places. With wide open spaces, the opportunity to interact with animals, ride on tractors or other farm equipment, swim in dams or lakes, get really dirty and stay that way all day, rural life really appeals to children of all ages. The chance to experience local farm produce and see where many foods come from is also hard to beat. And with less ambient light in the sky, the stars at night are something to behold, so stargazing is a must. And better still, with all the running around they are bound to do, no matter their age, you'll find they sleep soundly at night.

If you don't have access to a farm, take your child to an agricultural show for a taste of rural life, including a huge array of animals, demonstrations and some great rural produce. Or why not consider a farm stay next time you're planning the family holiday?

Fairs, fetes, shows and sales

Nearly every weekend, someone somewhere is organising a fair or fete celebrating everything from the best in organic food to excellence in arts and crafts. You are bound to find one that appeals to the entire family. My children and I love garage sales and car boot sales the best. You never know what you're going to find. It's like one huge lucky dip. Better still, many now give a percentage of their takings to local charities. Take a look in your local newspaper for listings, give your child some spare change and head off together to find some wonderful (and cheap) little treasures.

Botanic gardens and regional parks

With open spaces and so many interesting plants and interactive displays, botanic gardens and parks are the perfect place to run around, fly a kite, have a pony ride, enjoy a picnic, chase birds, lie under a tree, and get up close and personal with some truly awesome and rare plants.

Many Botanic Gardens offer excellent educational programs or workshops for preschoolers and primary-aged children. They play a critical role in educating children (gently) on issues such as sustainability, biodiversity, combating climate change and loss of plant habitats, thereby lessening the risk of kids developing ecophobia. Given that our children are being exposed to these issues more often, a visit to your local Botanic Garden can really help them begin to understand these important but bewildering issues. Encourage your older children to do some research on the Botanic clubs that are available to join online.

Easy lemon cordial

DIFFICULTY **2** MESS FACTOR **3** PREP TIME **30 MINS** COOKING TIME **2 HRS** MAKES **1.5 LITRES** APPROX.

750 ml lemon juice (Meyer lemons are the best for juice but are very pippy)

500 ml water

1 kg white sugar

This is a deliciously refreshing drink. Yes, it contains a lot of sugar, but if you make it a 'sometime' treat, it's a great addition to your picnic outings.

Method

Peel of around 3 lemons (sometimes we use limes too for more zing) – no pith please!

A drop of blue food dye (optional)

Pour the water and sugar into a large, deep saucepan and bring to the boil, stirring until all the sugar is dissolved. Add the peel, turn the heat down and simmer for around 40–50 minutes. The peel will start to look a bit funny at this stage but it's supposed to be like that.

Add the lemon juice, bring to the boil, stir and then reduce the heat again and simmer for a further 20 minutes. The mixture should have become lovely and syrupy. Take out the peel and allow to cool. If you wish, mix through a little food dye to make it a funky blue. Transfer to sterilised bottles or jars. Store in the fridge.

Munch, munch, pack a lunch

An outdoor picnic or barbecue never fails to thrill my children and they are now teenagers. Whether it's a full-scale production or a simple sandwich lunch on the grass in the front garden, they always love sharing their meal in the outdoors. Why not have a go at making some cordial to take along with you? (See previous page for recipe.)

Pack a hamper

Packing a hamper before you head off to explore the great outdoors can be great fun for everyone. There are so many delicious and easy foods you and your children can prepare: scones, pikelets, sandwiches, dips – and don't forget the old-fashioned but delicious scotch eggs (ask Grandma for the recipe!). We've included some recipes for three other yummy suggestions here. Your younger children will enjoy packing the hamper, filling the water bottles, folding up the picnic blanket and selecting the location. Older children might want to have a go at preparing the food.

Hummus

DIFFICULTY 2 MESS FACTOR 2 PREP TIME 15 MINS

COOKING TIME NIL FEEDS 4-6

400 g tin chickpeas, drained and rinsed

4 tablespoons tahini

2 garlic cloves, chopped

½ tsp ground cumin

Juice of 1 lemon

Salt and pepper to taste

1 tbsp extra virgin olive oil

Toasted sesame seeds for garnish

Method

Combine the chickpeas, tahini, garlic, cumin, lemon juice, and salt and pepper in a food processor and blitz until smooth. Taste for seasoning and adjust if necessary. If the hummus is too thick, you may need to add a little more lemon juice. Serve with extra virgin olive oil drizzled over the top. This is a very simple recipe that can be made by children 6+ by themselves if they are confident in the kitchen.

Potato salad

DIFFICULTY 2 MESS FACTOR 3 PREP TIME 30 MINS COOKING TIME 20 MINS FEEDS 8-10

6–7 Desiree potatoes, peeled and halved

1 cup whole-egg mayonnaise (more if you prefer)

5 hardboiled eggs, peeled and chopped

1 handful mixed fresh herbs (chives, parsley, lemon thyme)

1 handful of crispy bacon bits (optional)

Young children can help count out the potatoes and eggs. Once the eggs have cooked and cooled, the children can help peel the shells off. Three–five year olds can help dice the potatoes: size and shape don't matter. It will all taste good and the kids will have the best time tossing the salad in the bowl. Children 7+ can try this recipe by themselves.

Method

Cook the potatoes in boiling slightly salted water until just tender. Set aside to cool before dicing. Mix the potatoes, mayonnaise, eggs, bacon and herbs gently. Serve immediately.

Sweet potato and ricotta tart

DIFFICULTY 2 MESS FACTOR 2 PREP TIME 15 MINS COOKING TIME 40 MINS FEEDS 4-6

1 sweet potato (kumera), peeled and diced

60 g butter, melted

8 sheets filo pastry

500 g ricotta cheese

½ cup finely grated Parmesan cheese

2 eggs

¼ cup semi-dried tomatoes, finely diced

1 tbsp finely chopped flat leaf parsley

Salt and pepper

Younger children can help gather the ingredients from the fridge and pantry, pick the parsley from the garden, crack and whisk the eggs, brush each sheet of filo pastry with melted butter, then place the pastry in the tart tin and pour in the filling. Older children 7+ can have a go at this recipe by themselves.

Method

Preheat the oven to 180°C.

Cook sweet potato in boiling, slightly salted water for 5 mins or until tender. Drain well.

Melt the butter in a small saucepan. Brush each sheet of filo pastry with the butter. Line a 20 x 30 cm tart tin with the filo sheets, leaving the excess pastry to overhang the edges.

Combine the ricotta, Parmesan and eggs in a food processor and blitz until smooth. Spoon into a mixing bowl and fold in the sweet potato, semi-dried tomatoes and parsley and season with salt and pepper.

Place the filling on top of the pastry. Evenly cover the pastry with the mix.

Bake for 35 minutes or until the filling is set and golden. Serve with a green salad.

Fare for fairies

Help your young children make some simple sandwiches and chop up some fresh fruit and vegetables. If you have the time, you could consider making a butter cake (see page 21 for Simplicity cake recipe) and decorating it with pretty rosebuds and pink fairy floss. It is bound to be a hit with your children and the fairies. Don't forget to pack a few flowers, seeds, or pretty sticks and bits of grass for the elves, pixies or goblins that are sure to be lurking!

Find a shady spot in the garden or local park and lay out your picnic fare. Your children can put the lunch out for the fairies and goblins to find. Enjoy your lunch while you chat about when they will visit, how many will come and where they live. Return the next day and the fairy and goblin lunches are sure to be gone!

Snip! Snip!

This is a fun activity for children. When you feel your children are old enough to handle scissors or secateurs, you might encourage them to do a bit of pruning with you. Soft-stemmed plants are an ideal starting place for small children. Ask them to remove old flowers and, at the same time, encourage them to find a few nice ones for a vase.

You might like to buy a climbing frame from a garden centre — they come in interesting shapes and a plant suited to topiary and let your child clip away to their heart's content. Muehlenbeckia, Lonicera, Star Jasmine and some varieties of Buxus are good options. This is a great activity for younger children as it assists with fine motor skills.

GARDENING
– straight from the can

Gardening is one of the easiest ways I know of to get kids connected to the wonders of the outdoors.

Try this fun project. Wash with hot water some empty tin cans that once contained foods such as tomatoes, corn, beans, sprouts. Make sure you keep the outer labels on the can. Pierce a few holes into the bottom of the tin and fill with some quality potting mix. Now buy some seeds (or seedlings) of those plants that were used as the contents of the cans, i.e. a tomato seedling for the tomato can, a bean seed for the bean can, etc. This is a great lesson about food sources and can provide a pretty visual display for your windowsill.

GARDEN CENTRES

Garden centres are great to visit with kids. They are full of colour, movement, smells and of course plants! Your children will enjoy racing amongst all the different sorts of plants, helping you select them and putting them (or themselves) in the wheelbarrow or trolley.

The 'stinky' section (containing the fertilisers) is always of special interest to young children.

And, of course, there are all manner of useful and interesting things available that can be used for future outdoor activities. Bags of pebbles or sand, bits of bamboo and wooden stakes (think teepees and stakes for the veggie patch), fine wire and twine, child-safe garden tools, potted colour and seedlings, statuary and other garden décor.

Many large garden centres also have a coffee shop or café attached, so together you can enjoy a latte and muffin after hunting for the perfect herb.

Composting

Composting is fun, I promise! It's kind of like baking a cake over a three-month period, using fresh organic ingredients. Imagine your plants enjoying a delicious meal that's not only really good for them but will help them grow beautifully.

If you have the space and energy, you can build your own open compost heap, but this can be a space issue for most suburban backyards. So, the simplest way is to buy a turnable compost bin (readily available at most garden centres).

Before you start, it's important to know what you shouldn't put into your compost. This includes any kind of meat or fish (can attract vermin), citrus or onion (can turn the compost acidic and kill beneficial microorganisms), plastics, metal, tin or other non-biodegradable matter such as coated (or treated) paper, or cat or dog droppings (yuk). Also avoid an excess of ash from fireplaces. There is a specific recipe that you can follow in terms of quantities of each ingredient – a good mix of green waste (lawn clippings, fresh vegetation and kitchen scraps, but no weeds that contain seeds) and brown waste (dried garden matter such as small sticks, fallen leaves, etc.), a regular amount of water, some dolomite every now and then, and some manure (manure pellets or a 'compost starter'). Flip the bin regularly to circulate oxygen through the mix.

Check with your local nursery, online or with your local Botanic Garden for the perfect recipe for delectable compost. Yum!

making the most of each day

Worm farms

Did you know that Charles Darwin called worms 'Nature's Ploughs'?

For those with limited outdoor space, worm farms are fun and fairly easy for children to tend and maintain. They are relatively inexpensive to buy, but why not encourage your children to make their own? Like chooks and compost, worms are a great way to deal with kitchen scraps (again, no citrus, onion or meat).

Worms can be kept outside, inside, on a balcony or verandah, or in the garage. It's really important to avoid placing them in direct sunlight or you'll have roast worms in no time.

To make your worm farm you will need:

- three large, sturdy Styrofoam boxes, one with a lid (you can find these at your local greengrocer or butcher)
- shredded paper (non-coated and chemical-free)
- a bucketful of compost (you can buy a small bag from a garden centre if you don't yet have any of your own)
- compost worms – minimum 1000 (the regular garden varieties aren't suitable; you can buy composting worms from most garden centres or online)
- water
- kitchen scraps

Your children can do any part of this activity. Some might wish to wear gloves.

Ask your children to find an ideal spot for your worm farm and then place one of the Styrofoam boxes there.

Now poke some holes in the bottom of the second box (these are needed for drainage and aeration, but don't make them too big as you don't want the worms to drop through to the bottom box) and place it on top of the first empty box.

Put a layer (about 5 cm or so) of shredded paper mixed with a little compost on the bottom of the second box. Water until just moist.

Sprinkle your worms across the mix.

Add another layer of paper and compost. The box should be nearly full by now. Sprinkle with a little more water.

Poke some holes in the bottom of the third box and put it on top of the second box.

Put a layer of kitchen scraps into the top box and put the lid on.

You're done!

Wait a few days and add some more kitchen scraps to the top box. As a rule, you don't need to feed your worms more than twice a week. If the farm starts to smell yukky, you're probably adding too many scraps.

Your worms will tend to move up and down between the two top boxes (through the holes you've created) as they eat. Each worm can eat its own body weight each day. As they digest the scraps, they will produce worm wee and poo (known as castings). The goodness contained in these will fall/drain through into the bottom box where you'll eventually be able to harvest enough to use as excellent general-purpose fertiliser for your garden. Just make sure you dilute it with water until it looks a bit like weak tea. If your kids look after their worm farm, it can last for years.

making the most of each day

Here chook, chook, chook ...

Chooks have perky personalities, are great fun and relatively easy to keep. I have many friends who have become very attached to their hens; in fact, I've known some hens who sleep inside the family home. Not only do chooks produce fantastic fresh eggs, they are amongst the world's greatest insect hunters and will also keep some weeds at bay. Remember, however, to protect prized plants and watch out for the poos – they are prolific!

Happy roosting in a secure hen house overnight and roaming the garden (in a chicken run if necessary) during the day, chooks have minimal requirements. They don't need a vast amount of space; as a general rule of thumb, each chook needs about 4 square feet of its own in a coop/run. This will dictate how large your coop needs to be. (An A-Frame home is ideal.) It should have at least one roost, a fresh straw floor and two flaps: one to let your chooks in and out, the other to collect the eggs.

Chooks will happily devour your kitchen scraps (no meat please!) and need fresh water daily. Aim to have no more than six chooks in the average back garden and if you are in a highly urbanized area, remember the golden rule: no roosters. Although, personally, I long for the day when the cry of the lovelorn rooster once again echoes throughout the suburbs.

Chooks really are worth considering as part of developing a great organic food source for the family and a healthy outdoor environment for your children.

If you live in an urbanised area, it is best to check with your local council before buying chooks as they are bound to have certain rules and regulations on how they must be kept. Keeping and tending chooks is a project best suited to children 6+.

Keeping and tending chooks is a project best suited to children 6+.

VEGETABLE PATCHES

Why not consider building a simple veggie patch with your children? Not only will your family enjoy fresh fruits, vegetables and herbs throughout the year, the sense of achievement your children will experience when the first tomato or bean is picked will be worth the effort. To avoid disappointment and frustration, choose quick-growing plants with a high success rate, such as rocket/arugula, lettuce, radishes, beans and tomatoes. Pumpkins and zucchini always look spectacular in the patch but will tend to take over much of the space. If you have more than one child, you might like to split the garden bed in two and let them choose their own vegetables. If space is limited, many vegetables can be grown in pots by the back door or on a balcony.

Vegetable gardens can also be really silly! Strawberries look great planted into the back of an old toy truck and lettuce, pansies, petunias, French marigolds or violas look seriously cute planted in a pair of old boots or high heels — just make sure the container has adequate drainage holes and that your children check with you before raiding your shoe cupboard!

Jack, Jill and a bean stalk …

This is fun. Have each child plant a bean or pea seedling or seed (ensure you buy the climbing varieties) in the veggie patch or a large pot. Insert a stake or small teepee beside the plant and have a competition to see whose bean or pea plant reaches the top of the stake first. Your children might need to encourage the plant to twine around the stake, but once it's off and running, it will do this by itself. The rules are to have fun, give the plants regular love and attention and, if possible, seek no help from Mum or Dad. Your children will love taking responsibility for this project — and they will be more likely to start eating their greens!

Involve really little children, who may not have the patience for this level of gardening, by asking them to be the official 'picker' of the veggies. You might find that they begin to race out each morning to check whether the bean or pea vine has reached the top of the stake. It's a lovely sensory activity for them. Older children might like to devise a growth chart to track the progress of the plants.

making the most of each day

Container vegetable gardening

If space is at a premium, but there is room for some pots or a few wooden crates or Styrofoam boxes, you can still enjoy a vegetable garden. Just ensure your chosen containers have adequate drainage, a position that gets a good dose of sunshine each day, premium potting mix and mulch, and away you go. Good options to plant include tomatoes, beans, rocket/arugula, most herbs, capsicum/bell peppers, chillies/red peppers, carrots, spinach and lettuces. It's probably best to look for dwarf varieties where available.

The great thing about this method of gardening is that, depending on the size of your crates or boxes, your garden is pretty much portable. If you have a handyman in the family, have him/her attach some small wheels or casters to your containers so there's no need to lift them – simply wheel them about when and if you need to!

Egg and herb pasta

DIFFICULTY **4** MESS FACTOR **3** PREP TIME **30 MINS** COOKING TIME **20 MINS** FEEDS **6**

3-4 cups of your child's favourite pasta

1 tbsp olive oil

6 bacon rashers, chopped

Medium sprig of curly parsley, roughly chopped

Medium sprig of basil, roughly chopped

Small handful of chives, roughly chopped

2 garlic cloves, minced

One punnet of grape tomatoes chopped in half lengthways

1 cup cream

2 eggs, lightly beaten

¾ cup grated tasty or Parmesan cheese

Your young child can choose their favourite pasta shape and help measure the quantities, as well as gather the other ingredients from the fridge, pantry and garden. Your child's like or dislike of 'green' will determine how many herbs you might choose to plant and use. Children 7+ can have a go at this recipe by themselves.

Method

Cook the pasta in boiling, slightly salted water until *al dente*, drain and return to the pot. Keep warm.

Heat the olive oil in a fry pan over medium heat, add the bacon, half the herbs, tomatoes and garlic and cook until the bacon is just beginning to crisp and the garlic is just starting to soften. Turn off the heat and allow the mix to cool slightly.

Add the cream, stir well and combine with the pasta. Pour the eggs over the pasta and mix through while the pasta is still hot. Add the cheese, garnish with the remaining herbs and serve immediately.

WATERING THE GARDEN

NO-GARDEN GARDENS

If you don't have a garden at all, why not consider taking on a public allotment or joining a community garden program? Many councils and nurseries now have public space set aside for just this purpose, and some are free.

Watering the garden can be pretty monotonous for adults and, sadly, the days of running under the sprinkler on a summer's day are regularly restricted due to water scarcity/drought. But this doesn't mean our children should miss out on the excitement and sensory pleasure of water play. With a bit of forward planning, the back garden can once again become a watery wonderland.

Start by storing containers at your back door (make sure they have lids so they're not a drowning hazard or breeding ground for mosquitoes). When it rains, ask your child to place them outside to catch as much water as possible.

Similarly, when they or another family member takes a shower, encourage your children to put some buckets in the shower to collect the water before it runs down the plughole. It's amazing how quickly they fill up. Together, transfer them outside and, using plastic cups and jars or watering cans, let them splash away, pouring the water from container to container. This simple act delights a young child and assists with both fine and gross motor skills. Also, fill up a water sprayer and encourage them to water the nearby plants and themselves.

Add some food dye to a few of the containers (preferably clear so the children can see the water changing colour) and let them make rainbow water – although you might want to hide the water sprayer at this point unless you want dyed children and clothing!

Using their bathwater can also be fun. If it's not a total mass of bubbles (which may harm your plants), it can be used to water the garden, wash the dog or car, or remove some stains from paving.

making the most of each day

Mushroom risotto

DIFFICULTY **4** MESS FACTOR **4** PREP TIME **15 MINS** COOKING TIME **30–40 MINS** FEEDS **6**

1 tbsp dried porcini mushrooms

1 large knob of butter

1 large brown onion, peeled and finely diced (if your child does the dicing, encourage them to wear swimming goggles)

2 cups quality Arborio rice

Up to 2 litres warmed quality chicken or vegetable stock

150 g mushrooms from your kit, roughly chopped

300 g exotic mushrooms such as pine, enoki, shitake, pink oyster – all roughly chopped

1 cup Parmesan cheese

Zest of half a lemon

Chilli flakes (optional)

1 bunch of chervil, half for the recipe, half for garnish

Salt and pepper

My children have adored this version of risotto since they were tiny. Today, as teenagers, they still often request it when their friends are coming to stay or on other special occasions. I encourage you to give it a try. I always feel a bit of a fraud as people seem to think it's complicated, but it's really super easy – this is my promise to you!

Younger children can help by collecting all the ingredients and placing them on the kitchen bench because it is preferable, for any risotto recipe, that you have all your ingredients prepared and ready to go before you start cooking.

Older children 9+ can try this recipe on their own if you are comfortable with their level of proficiency in the kitchen.

Method

Put the dried porcini mushrooms in a measuring cup and fill it with boiling water (1 cup worth of fluid). Set aside to infuse.

Heat the butter in a large, flat casserole dish or fry pan until melted. Add the onion and cook until just softened. Add the rice and stir through until it is completely coated with the butter and onion.

Add the stock gradually, a soup ladle at a time. After each addition, stir the rice until the liquid is almost absorbed. You will see the rice beginning to swell and soften after you've done this a few times. Once you've used half the stock, add the mushrooms (all but the porcini) and stir through the rice until combined.

Continue to add the stock, one ladle at a time, until you have run out. You may find that you don't need all the stock. ~ Taste the rice – by now it should be almost cooked. If that's the case, no more stock is required.

Add half of the Parmesan, lemon zest, half of the chervil, chilli flakes (if desired), a good crack of black pepper and a large pinch of salt, and stir until they are well combined in the risotto.

Add the porcini mushrooms (and the water in which they have been soaking) and continue to stir until the rice is cooked. It should be soft with a creamy texture.

Serve immediately in large bowls. Garnish with the remaining Parmesan and chervil. Delicious!

MUSHROOM KITS

Want fresh vegetables that your children can harvest all through the year and that don't need a garden? Then you'll want a mushroom kit.

Mushrooms are the easiest things my children and I have ever grown. The kits are available for sale throughout the year. Simply put the kit somewhere with minimal light and no draughts (garage, laundry, linen cupboard are ideal), keep cool and moist, but not wet, and within approximately two weeks, your children will be able to harvest their first crop.

A quality mushroom kit will supply mushrooms for between 4–8 weeks. The kits come with full instructions. The added bonus is that, after the kit is spent, the contents make beautiful natural fertiliser for your potted or garden plants (avoid placing on roses, azaleas or gardenias). You can find kits at many garden centres, mushroom farms or via the internet.

Use it again!

Some children are natural hoarders, which is a great trait when it comes to helping them learn about the value of recycling. Encourage children to think about using things again rather than tossing everything away or expecting new things all the time. Here's a list of everyday objects you and your children can recycle for use either in the garden or for fun craft activities:

- the <u>really</u> annoying bits of plastic-coated wire (used on toy packaging)
- food scraps (if you have a compost heap, chooks or a worm farm)
- leaf litter and other garden waste (return them to your garden or compost heap)
- cardboard boxes, cardboard, unbleached paper and old envelopes (for craft activities or for making the perfect train, bus, boat, car or board game)
- old newspapers (can be spread over garden beds to suppress weeds or used to stuff scarecrows)
- plastic bottles, containers of all shapes and sizes, cans (perfect for water play and other outdoor craft activities such as maracas, wind chimes and rain gauges)
- egg cartons (perfect for growing little cresses and other sweet plants)
- old toys (can be used as pots for plants)
- string, twine, old ribbons (for use in attaching, tying and hanging craft treasures)
- used espresso coffee pods
- empty toilet and paper towel rolls (instant imaginary magnifying glasses, good for catching insects, for use as imaginary swords and sabers and for other general craft activities)
- sticks and interesting branches, gumnuts and seed pods, feathers, shells, pebbles and other stones, fallen bark, fallen discarded birds' nests (for use in a wide range of outdoor craft activities or to add to found collections).

Be aware that some of the above may pose a choking risk.

indoor activities

For some, regular access to large outdoor spaces is difficult, and at times even those with outdoors aplenty will not want to open the front door, much less venture out. So why not consider bringing the outdoors in? There are many fun things you can do in a small space or when it's raining.

You might decide that you'll hunt only for 'old' things. Search for the oldest living tree in existence, or the largest. Try and find out where the first dinosaur bone was discovered. Dig out a few pictures of great-great grandpa or search for the oldest thing you can find in your house. This activity is best enjoyed by children 6+.

If you do decide to venture out when the weather is inclement, museums, art galleries, aquariums and libraries have jam-packed schedules of activities for young children. Don't overlook these as an alternative to staying indoors.

Pet rock collection

Rocks, stones and pebbles in every conceivable shape and size are a ready resource and can be found almost anywhere. They are also great fun to collect. Encourage your child to start his own collection. You'll be amazed at what he can find – even if access to outdoors is limited. A fishing tackle box is an ideal place for the collection. For those that become special, your child might like to think up a name and write it on the rock. Or he may decide to sort them by shape, texture, colour or size, or create several families of rocks.

Consider taking truly precious treasures to an engraver and having a word of your child's choice etched onto the stone.

Online and TV delights If regular visits to cultural institutions are difficult, you might consider encouraging your child to visit them online. Some run terrific membership programs, including great kids' clubs. Free magazines, newsletters, postcards, stickers, bookmarks and activity packs may all be on offer. You can also help children Google outdoor images on your computer for use in a scrapbook or as a part of indoor craft play.

If watching television is a favourite activity, interspersing their favourite program with the National Geographic channel or a free-to-air program on nature, gardening, animals or exotic holiday destinations can really fire little imaginations.

Egg carton delights

Your child can grow (and eventually eat) some really cute little plants in an old egg carton. I like alfalfa sprouts, mung beans and a selection of cresses as they only need a tiny container in which to grow. You could grow some sweet little violas, too.

Simply have your child fill each space in the carton with a little sandy potting mix, then sprinkle a few seeds in and cover very slightly with the mix. Remember not to overcrowd the seeds. Place them on a sunny windowsill and keep moist, but not wet (so the egg carton doesn't disintegrate). Using a water mister is a good option.

For a bit of a twist, you can sit empty eggshells in an egg carton or egg cup and fill them with potting mix. Violas look particularly gorgeous sprouting from an old eggshell!

Nature's journal

Encourage your child to begin a nature journal. Start by having them sit at a window and draw whatever they see. It might be the family cat lying contentedly in a shaft of sunlight, the neighbour's washing line, a lavender shrub or some billowing clouds racing by. Rainbows are always a popular subject. The sketches may be nothing more than a few squiggles and a splash of colour to begin with.

When your children do venture out, suggest they take their journal with them and record what they see around them. They can collect little bits and pieces to stick in the journal to remind them of their time outside. They can also take photos and pop them into the journal too.

Older children might like to choose one subject and record all they can about it. For example, they could focus only on the vegetable patch and record growth habits and harvest times, or they could record all the different types of clouds they observe, or they might want to research the birds of your neighbourhood. Your child may become quite attached to their journal as it slowly becomes the repository of thoughts, dreams, tender drawings and little gems from nature. This activity will be enjoyed most by children aged five and over. My daughter, now 13 still has her nature journal and adds to it every now and then.

weedy head

If you have an old stocking (without a reinforced toe) to hand, your child can make a Grass Man. All they need to do is fill the toe of a stocking with sawdust and grass seed (rye grass is ideal) to form a round ball (put the grass seeds in first and backfill with the sawdust). Snip the stocking to shorten and secure with a rubber band, then have your child draw a face on the ball with permanent markers. Fill a cup or round container with water and place the stocking ball (grass seed side facing up) on top so it fits snugly. Put in a sunny spot and keep well watered. Within a few weeks the little man will begin to grow hair. Your child will enjoy giving him a variety of different kooky haircuts. You can also use edible cresses for this project.

making the most of each day

Grandma Joyce's scones

DIFFICULTY 1 MESS FACTOR 3 PREP TIME 15 MINS COOKING TIME 20 MINS MAKES 12–15

3 cups self-raising flour

60 g salted butter, chopped

1 tsp caster sugar (optional)

Tiny pinch of salt

1½ cups milk

Whipped cream and jam

Method

Preheat oven to 200°C. Line a flat baking tray with greaseproof baking paper. You can dust a little plain flour over the paper if you wish.

Sift the self-raising flour into a large bowl and add the butter and sugar. Now your child can rub the butter through the flour until it looks like breadcrumbs. Have them make a well in the centre of the mix and pour the milk gently into the well. Mix to combine using a flat wooden spoon. The mixture will now look like a soft dough.

Put the dough onto a flat surface dusted with some plain flour (a wooden chopping board is ideal) and gently knead it. Don't go overboard with your kneading, otherwise the scones will be hard and rubbery once cooked.

Form the dough into a flattish circle (about an inch thick). Using the open end of a small drinking glass or cookie cutter, cut out circles from the dough. You can brush them with a little milk if you wish, as this will make them lovely and shiny on top. Pop them onto your baking tray and bake in the oven for around 20 minutes or until they have risen and the tops are starting to turn golden.

Take them out of the oven and cool slightly on a cake rack. Serve them with dollops of whipped cream and jam of your child's choice. Yum!

When I was little I used to love visiting Grandma and cooking with her in the kitchen. We'd make all sorts of old-fashioned dishes such as totally delicious chocolatey custard, tuna mornay, beer and beef casseroles, apple or rhubarb crumble, trifles and syllabub – and we'd nearly always bake a cake from scratch. She also used to save the water she'd cooked our vegetables in and pour it into a large mug, add a tiny knob of butter and a little salt and give it to us as a delicious consommé before our main meal. She believed that all the goodness went out of the vegetables and into the cooking water! I doubt it, but the resulting clear soup was quite delicious.

But by far my favourite food was her scones. I encourage you to let your child have a go at this recipe. They make a perfect afternoon tea or addition to a picnic hamper. Children under 5 will be your assistants; children 6+ can have a go at this by themselves.

FAMILY TREE

Making a visual family tree is fun and more easily understood by young ones than its written counterpart.

With your children, collect some largish leafless branches that look like mini trees. Using coloured string or ribbon, help your children to tie their favourite photos or drawings of their family to the branches (scan or photocopy them if you don't want to use the originals). Start with Grandpa and Grandma and work your way down the tree. Don't forget the family pets. Use a small bucket of sand to hold the tree in place. If you can't find a real branch for this activity, consider having your child draw a tree instead, leaving spaces where they can attach pictures of their family.

Ant farms

Unless you want ants crawling through your honey, your child's Lego® or along the ceiling, a store-bought sealed ant farm really is the only option if you wish to investigate the fascinating world of ants. They're relatively cheap and easy to maintain.

Ants are such industrious little creatures – they never seem to stop – and children delight in watching them. The fact that they can see underground also really appeals.

FLOWER PRESSING

Though considered an old-fashioned activity by some, young children really enjoy this easy pastime.

Choose flowers that are simple in their arrangement (a daisy, viola or any other single-petalled flower is ideal) and not too fleshy. Put the flower gently between two pieces of paper towel or unbleached tissue paper, spreading the petals out, then place into a book. Close the book, place a stack of other books on top and leave for about a month. By then, the flower should be flat and dry and perfect for use in craft activities or to make a sweet little picture that you might wish to have framed.

making the most of each day

Seasons

Spring

Summer

Autumn

WInter

Getting outside with Mother Nature and observing the changes she brings every few months provides some fabulous lessons about the world around us.

Every year she offers up the most wonderful stories about birth, growth, beauty and death. What better way to help your children understand the magic of nature than by getting outdoors and observing the seasons?

spring

Everything is bursting with life during spring. The blossoms of deciduous trees put on a spectacular display, and there are fresh hues of green popping up everywhere. Bulbs explode from the ground and provide a carpet of blooms just waiting to be sat amongst or picked for a pretty indoor arrangement. Young lambs are bleating, magpies and mockingbirds are attacking and the weather is warming up. All in all, it's a really exciting time for young children to be out and about observing.

Spring, spring is coming soon
Grass is green and flowers bloom
Birds returning from the south
Bees are buzzing all about
Leaves are budding everywhere
Spring, spring is finally here!

Unknown

What to eat

Asparagus, broad beans, chives, coriander/cilantro, dill, Dutch carrots, garden peas, globe artichokes, marjoram, mint, oregano, parsley, radishes, rhubarb, rocket/arugula, rosemary (new growth), sage, spring onions, strawberries, tarragon, thyme, watercress, zucchini/courgette flowers.

What to plant

Aloe vera, basil, bay tree, beans, beetroot, buxus, cantaloupe/rockmelon, capsicum/bell pepper, carrots, catmint, catnip, celery, chervil, chillies/red peppers, corn, Cosmos, cucumber, cumquat, dill, eggplant/aubergine, fennel, French marigolds, hippeastrum (early), lemon, lemon thyme, lemon verbena, lettuce, lime, marjoram, mint, mushroom kits, nasturtium, onions, oranges, oregano, parsley, pineapple, sage, potatoes, pumpkin/squash, radishes, rhubarb, rocket/arugula, rosemary, sage, silverbeet /chard, strawberries, sunflowers, Tagetes (seed), tarragon, thyme, tomatoes, watermelon, Wollemi pine, zucchini /courgette.

Artichoke dip

DIFFICULTY 2 MESS FACTOR 3 PREP TIME 10 MINS COOKING TIME 10 MINS FEEDS 10

2 x 400 g tins artichoke hearts in water, drained

2/3 cup grated Gruyere cheese

2/3 cup grated Parmesan cheese

2/3 cup whole-egg mayonnaise

Dash of Tabasco sauce

2 tablespoons finely chopped dill

1 tsp paprika

This dip is delicious for picnics or any social gathering. Older children can have a go at this recipe by themselves.

Method

Preheat the oven to 180°C.

Place the artichokes, gruyere, Parmesan, mayonnaise, Tabasco and dill in a food processor and blend until smooth.

Spoon the mixture into an ovenproof bowl, sprinkle with the paprika and place in the oven for 10 minutes. Serve warm with salty crackers.

seasons

PART 3

Globe artichokes

DIFFICULTY 3 MESS FACTOR **2** PREP TIME **10 MINS** COOKING TIME **30 MINS** FEEDS **4**

4 whole, fresh
globe artichokes

30 g butter, melted

1 lemon, juiced

Pepper and salt

Globe artichokes herald spring. My children love the look of this funky plant (it's a relative of the thistle), and enjoy the tactile sensation of pulling off the leaves, scooping out the heart and sucking the flesh with butter running down their fingers. Children 7+ can help with nearly all of this recipe. Younger ones might just like to observe and eat!

Method

Harvest (or buy) a few fresh globe artichokes. Cut the stem so only a few centimetres remain where the base of the leaves begin. Then cut through the top of leaves so around two-thirds of the total globe remains. Remove a couple of the outer layers of the leaves.

Place the remaining artichoke into some rapidly boiling salted water. Cook for 20–25 minutes, or until the stem is soft and tender.

Remove from the water, drain and allow to cool until you can handle it comfortably with your hands. Prise the leaves apart. In the centre, you will find the 'heart' of the artichoke. This needs to be removed by gently scooping out the fibrous straw-like husk.

Arrange the artichokes in a small round bowl, drizzle with a little melted butter and some lemon juice, and top with freshly cracked black pepper and sea salt (or have these on the side to dip into).

Now eat! Working from the outside leaves to the inner, pull off and suck the flesh from the bottom of the leaf. The further you go the leaves become more tender – you'll probably find you can eat the last few whole. You can also eat the stem and the base. Delicious!

MAGPIE AND MOCKINGBIRD MADNESS Many birds are actively nesting with their young during spring. You can find them by watching for heightened activity in the trees and listening for the calls they will be making to each other. Grab some binoculars and head out with your children to take a look. Try and identify the birds and together draw pictures of them when you get home. Older children might like to head to the computer and do some research on the birds of your neighbourhood.

Magpies and mockingbirds are particularly protective of their young and can feel very threatened when a human happens to wander into their territory. In fact, they can seem positively crazy! They will swoop, screech and generally try to scare the wits out of you. Their beaks are sharp and can really hurt an unprotected head or damage an eye. Our experience recommends steering clear of this bird until the nesting season is over or wear protective headwear and safety glasses – which can be fun in itself!

Blossom watch

Take a walk with your child around your suburb, farm or community and look at the variety of blossoms on offer. As the blossoms begin to fall, together, collect as many as you can. Return home and put them in a small container or basket. Add a few cotton wool balls for pillows and a tiny piece of fabric or ribbon, or one big, fat, soft green leaf, for a blanket. Take the basket/container outside and offer it to the fairies as a spring blossom bed. If you want to help fire your child's imagination a little more, at night when they are sleeping place a tiny thank-you note in the basket.

Older children could also have a go at pressing the blossoms (see page 65) or make a picture of a tree, flower or shrub with the pressed blossoms as part of a craft activity. Children 9+ could do some research on how many types of blossoms there are, why trees blossom and in what order a tree grows leaves, blossoms and fruit.

seasons

baby leaf birds

After scouting your neighbourhood for real baby birds, you might want to encourage your children to make their own! You will need:

- a collection of small leaves, small sticks, bark, small dried berries or currants
- a selection of feathers (bought or found)
- a few blocks of Oasis® (rigid foam) or a roll of tin foil
- PVA or craft glue
- some white or neutral-coloured tissue paper (or colours of your choice)
- flexible thin bits of wire such as plastic-coated or thick fuse wire, or pipe cleaners
- gold or silver glitter spray (optional).
- Collect a variety of things from outside to make a body, eyes and a beak (such as small spring leaves, small sticks, bark and berries, or feathers)

When home, sit outside and carve the Oasis® or scrunch tin foil into the shape of a bird's body. (The Oasis® is easy to carve, so young children can do this using a blunt knife.)

Once you and your children are happy with the general shape, cover the body with glue and then with a few layers of tissue paper (torn into small, manageable pieces).

Wait for the glue and tissue paper to dry, then glue on the small leaves. Have them all face the same way so they begin to resemble feathers. Use real feathers to make the wings and tail feather. Attach the beak and eyes.

Finally, twist two bits of wire or pipe cleaner (you could also use small sticks or toothpicks) until they resemble birds' feet. It's fun for the children to twist, untwist and twist again. When they're happy with the feet, insert them into the Oasis® or foil and arrange them so the bird can stand.

Don't forget the zoo!

Many zoo animals may have given birth to their young by now. It's well worth taking a trip to check out what's going on. Some zoos also offer great night walks and fun sleepovers for kids (and parents), with opportunities to interact with the animals at dusk and dawn.

PREDATOR WATCH

With many plants actively growing in spring, the insect and animal population is on the lookout for a tender snack of sweet new leaves, juicy twining tendrils and irresistible buds.

While it may be incredibly annoying for you, and heartbreaking for your children, to find your spinach demolished overnight or the new tendrils of your beans reduced to a stump, it's also important that we begin to teach children about the importance of all creatures in our ecosystems and general web of life. That said, here are a few ideas on ways to move our garden predators along (permanently) the natural way.

Drunk Snails

Snails and slugs can cause terrible problems in the garden. Although, if you have chooks or are lucky enough to have a resident blue tongue lizard, you probably don't need to make snails drunk. Drunk, you say?

Ask your children to pour a little beer into a small plastic dish (an empty plastic butter container without its lid is ideal). Place it in the garden near your vulnerable plants, so it can't tip over. The snails, attracted to the malty smell, will make a beeline for it. Their slimy cousins, the less attractive slug, may also stop by. They'll all be dead by morning.

Companion Planting

This is a term used to describe plants that benefit from being planted beside one another, either because they assist each other in growing, or one acts as a natural repellent for the predators that find its companion attractive. Other plants, regardless of who their neighbours are, will also repel insects.

- Basil plants repel white fly, which in turn loves tomatoes, so try planting them together. They are also yummy when eaten together!
- Garlic and chives planted around roses can help with aphids and black spot.
- Not only is lavender beautifully fragrant and attractive to butterflies, it also repels mice, ticks and some moths. Mint has the same effect.
- Nasturtium, which is very easy to grow, is an all-round insect repellent for many vegetables such as broccoli, cabbage and cauliflower, so a must for any vegetable or kitchen garden.
- The humble scented marigold is a great deterrent. It keeps the soil free of horrid nematodes and attracts many beneficial insects to the garden. It's a must-have plant in your herb garden (the flowers and leaves are edible). French marigolds (the types that are small and dainty-looking) help send white flies packing when planted around tomatoes.

seasons

summer

Shimmering heat, juicy summer fruits, holiday treats and visits to the beach – summer is the ultimate sensory season.

It's almost impossible not to find a reason to head outside during summer. There's so much for children to do and see. It's a sensory season, full of new sounds, overripe smells and dizzying heat. It's the time to eat fresh summer fruits and perfectly ripe avocadoes, run around under the sprinkler the back garden in the 'nud', listen to evening thunderstorms boom over the neighbourhood and, of course, step barefoot on a Bindii.

The summer sun's come out to play
And we can stay outside all day!
Juicy fruits and ice creams galore,
It's the best time to be at the seashore
So please stay with us summer sun
We're going to have some awesome fun!

Caro Webster

What to eat

Apricots, avocadoes, bananas, basil, beetroot, blueberries, cantaloupe/rockmelon, capsicum/bell pepper, carrots, cherries, chillies/red pepper, corn, cucumber, eggplant/aubergine, English spinach, garlic, green beans, hearted lettuce (cos, iceberg etc.), loganberries, lychees, mangoes, nectarines, peaches, raspberries, rocket/arugula, snow peas, strawberries, sugar snaps, tomatoes, watermelon, zucchini/courgette.

What to plant

Aloe vera, azaleas, bananas, basil, bay tree, beans, beetroot, Buxus, cantaloupe/rockmelon, capsicum/bell pepper, carrots, celery, chillies, corn, Cosmos, cucumbers, eggplant/aubergine, lavender, lemon grass, lemon verbena, marigolds, mushroom kits, oregano, petunias, pumpkin/squash, sunflowers, tomatoes, watermelon, Wollemi pine, zucchini/courgette.

Children's fish cakes

DIFFICULTY **2** MESS FACTOR **5** PREP TIME **15 MINS** COOKING TIME **20 MINS** MAKES **10**

4 potatoes, peeled and diced

350 g tuna or salmon, pin-boned and chopped into small pieces

1 carrot, peeled and grated

3 eggs

4–6 green onions, finely chopped

Salt and pepper

½ cup plain flour

1 cup breadcrumbs

2 tbsps vegetable oil

Young children (3–5) can assist by gathering the ingredients, cracking and whisking the eggs, peeling the carrot (some may attempt grating) and rolling the mixture into balls. Children 6+ can have a go at this recipe by themselves.

Method

Cook the potatoes in boiling, slightly salted water for 6 minutes or until just tender. Drain and mash.

Combine the potato, fish, carrot, 1 egg, green onions and salt and pepper in a bowl and mix well. Cover and place in the fridge for 30 minutes. Remove mixture from fridge and roll into balls or flat discs.

Lightly beat the remaining eggs in a bowl. Place the flour and breadcrumbs in separate shallow bowls. Coat the fish cakes in flour, then in the beaten egg and lastly in the breadcrumbs.

Heat the oil in a fry pan over medium heat, add the fish cakes, in batches, and shallow fry on each side for 3 minutes or until golden and cooked through.

seasons

Summer Pavlova

DIFFICULTY **3** MESS FACTOR **3** PREP TIME **20 MINS** COOKING TIME **1 HR** AND ADDITIONAL **1 HR** RESTING TIME

FEEDS **6-10** DEPENDING ON HOW THICK YOUR SLICES ARE!

6 egg whites

1 cup caster sugar

1 tsp vanilla extract

1–2 tsps cornflour (optional) –
'It supposedly makes the Pavlova glossier.'

500 ml thickened cream

1 punnet each of strawberries, blackberries, raspberries and blueberries

My daughter has been making Pavlova since she was about six. This pleases me greatly because it is a divine mix of gooey marshmallow on the inside, crunchy meringue on the outside and lashings of whipped cream, with a mass of summer berries plopped on top. It truly is one of the best and easiest desserts ever. And if on the off chance it doesn't work out perfectly, just gently smash it up and you have instant Eton Mess. Children under six will be helpers with this dessert. Depending on their confidence in the kitchen, children 7+ can have a go at it by themselves. Separating the egg white from the yolk is probably the only thing they might need a little help with.

This is my daughter's recipe word for word.

Method

Preheat the oven to 160°C. Make sure the oven setting is on conventional, not fan-forced. Line a flat tray with baking paper. Make sure the tray is big enough to fit a dollop of meringue about 15–20 cm. in diameter.

Separate the 6 eggs into bowls. Keep the yolks to make some mayonnaise, a super- rich (but delicious) omelette or an egg flip! Put the egg whites into a food processor and beat until soft peaks form. Add the sugar and cornflour gradually, continuing to beat with each addition. Add the vanilla extract.

Once the meringue is a little bit stiff and glossy, scoop it onto the tray and smooth out the mixture with a spatula to make a disc-like shape. Don't let Mum lick the bowl.

Place in the oven for 1 hour. Once you have finished cooking the Pavlova, turn off the oven and leave it in the oven. DO NOT OPEN THE OVEN! Leave it there for 60 minutes.

Now take the cooled Pavlova out of the oven, whip some cream and layer it on top and then top generously with fresh fruit of your own choice. My Mum loves summer red berries best.

beach art

This is a great activity when you're at the beach. Remember to take sunscreen, hats and water to drink.

After the building of sandcastles, swimming, hunting in rock pools, and collecting seaweed and shells is over, have your child think of a simple object to draw in the sand. It could be a mermaid, a fish, a happy face, a shell, or their name. Using a piece of driftwood, a bucket and spade or simply your hands, together draw a gigantic version of their chosen object. Use the seaweed and other objects to decorate it. If possible, do the drawing in a place where it can be viewed from above. Make sure they take their marine collection home to add to their found collection.

Fishing

Those who love fishing are really passionate about it. It's a great way for children to spend time with a parent, grandparent or a special person in their life. You could go on a day trip and take a picnic lunch. Be prepared though – it's both relaxing and frustrating. Patience is key!

Fishing is an excellent way to teach children the value of waiting for a result, even though it may not always be the result they anticipated. The thrill, however, of catching their first fish is something that will long be remembered – so have a camera at hand. To this day, I remember my son, aged five, catching a poor little bream. Big enough to keep, we scaled and gutted him (yuk!) and ate him for dinner that night. Before this, I think my son thought all fish came ready-crumbed, out of a packet and were shaped like a finger! His love of fishing remains to this day.

There are many types of fishing and lots of rules and regulations that come with them, so check your area's licence requirements, size and bag limits, and protected species. Or if your child would rather not go fishing, how about taking them to your local fish market? Here, they will see an incredible variety of fish and shellfish, providing another lesson on food sources, and the smells are truly amazing. If you arrive early enough, you might see the fishermen (usually accompanied by a cloud of sea birds) returning with their catch of the day.

float your boat

. . .

When you are out and about with your children, look for large leaves or branches that can be used as a boat. The stems of fallen palm leaves (especially the Bangalow Palm) are ideal.

The very ends of these, when cut from the frond, make a perfect boat. You will need a small saw to cut through the fibrous stem, then leave it to your children to decorate their new cruising vessel. They can use pencils, pens, glitter and acrylic-based paints to decorate the boat and small stones, or whatever is to hand, for the passengers. They can also write its name on the side of the boat.

Together, head to a duck pond, a still beach, the backyard pool or the bath. For a bit of fun, have a naming ceremony and launch the vessel with great fanfare. If launching into the ocean, consider putting a message in a bottle inside the boat.

Pea risotto

DIFFICULTY 3 MESS FACTOR **3** PREP TIME **15 MINS** COOKING TIME **30-40 MINS** FEEDS **6**

1 large knob of butter

1 large leek, finely sliced (white part only)

1½ cups quality Arborio rice

Up to 2 litres warmed quality chicken or vegetable stock

150 g fresh, podded garden peas

150 g sugar or snow peas/mangetout, sliced thinly lengthwise

1 small packet frozen baby peas

⅔ cup Parmesan cheese for the pot, ⅓ for garnish

Bunch of mint, half for the recipe, half for garnish

A few sprigs of thyme or lemon thyme (leaves only)

Chilli flakes (optional)

Zest of half a lemon

Salt and pepper

Risotto scares some people, as they think it's a tricky dish to master. But I don't subscribe to that view at all. As long as you have all your ingredients ready to go before you start and are prepared to spend a little time standing over your pot stirring, a basic risotto is relatively easy to cook and a very good dish for older children to add to their kitchen repertoire. Once they understand the basics of risotto, they can make any number of variations of this humble dish. Pea Risotto is a good starting point for children 7+ to try on their own if you are comfortable with their level of proficiency in the kitchen. Younger children can help by collecting all the ingredients and placing them on the kitchen bench. See page 58 for a mushroom version.

Method

In a large flat casserole dish or deep fry pan, heat the butter until melted. Add the leek and cook until just softened. Add the rice and stir through until it is completely coated with the butter and leek. Gradually, a soup ladle at a time, add the stock

After each addition, stir the rice until the liquid is almost absorbed. You will see the rice beginning to swell and soften after you've done this a few times. Once you've used half the stock, add the peas and stir through the rice until combined.

Continue to add the stock, one ladle at a time. You may find that you don't need all the stock. Taste the rice – by now it should be almost cooked. If that's the case, no more stock is required.

Now add half of the Parmesan, half of the mint and all of the thyme, chilli (if using), lemon zest, a good crack of black pepper and a large pinch of salt and stir until they are well combined through the risotto. The rice should be soft with a creamy texture.

Serve immediately in large bowls. Garnish with the remaining Parmesan and mint. Delicious!

Yummy yabbies

If you live in the country, why not try your hand at landing a yabby or other freshwater crustacean? Many dams and creeks/rivers will be bursting with yabbies in the summer months. It's best to head out in the early morning or evening.

You can buy a yabby trap, but it's much more fun for children (and cheaper) to attach some raw meat (which, I'm afraid, must be slightly pongy) to a bit of string, throw it in the dam and wait. Patience is needed, but when you see the line move or go taut, pull it in quickly, but methodically, and use a net to snare the yabby. Once your children are satisfied with their haul, head to the kitchen.

If you think your children can cope with the cooking process, have them assist. Bring a large pot of salted water to a hard boil and quickly tip the yabbies in, watching out for their nippers. Cook until they turn red (around 5–10 minutes). Some will squeal. Reassure your children that it's not the yabby screaming, just the air escaping their exoskeleton as their flesh expands – still a wretched thought! Some people put the yabbies in the freezer for half an hour or so before cooking them, but it's my view that this only extends their misery.

Remove the yabbies from the pot and arrange on a large platter, chop up some limes and serve with crunchy bread and a salad. You may need to help your children peel the cooked yabbies as the shell is harder than that of a prawn or shrimp.

I like to drizzle them with a little melted butter, a squeeze of lime, a sprinkle of freshly torn herbs (chervil, parsley, lemon thyme or chives) and some cracked pepper. Avoid salt, as you've already cooked them in salted water.

autumn/fall

Leaves to stomp through, brilliant colours everywhere, blustery showers of rain and the beginnings of glorious puddles. There's so much to see and do, so grab a scarf and head outdoors!

In autumn/fall, Mother Nature puts on a spectacular outdoor display. When the days are crisp and clear, the sky can appear impossibly blue. Deciduous plants prepare for their winter rest; their leaves change colour and then fall from the tree completely. The result? A dazzling display of colour throughout your suburb and nearby botanic gardens, parks and forests.

Children enjoy collecting leaves at this time. With every colour from grubby browns, light and vibrant yellows and dusky purples through to eye-popping scarlets and reds, now is the time to do some colouring in! The leaves can be used to great effect in craft activities. Many plants will also have a good display of berries, which can look beautiful indoors in a vase. Rosehips are particularly pretty. Remember to watch for berries inadvertently being popped into the mouth by a little one. All can be potentially toxic or pose a choking risk.

They're coming down in showers,
The leaves all gold and red;
They're covering the little flowers,
And tucking them in bed
They've spread a fairy carpet
All up and down the street;
And when we skip along to school,
they rustle 'neath our feet

Winifred C Marshall ~ (1761-1839)

What to eat

Apples, beetroot, blackberries, cabbages, cauliflower, celeriac, figs, grapes, Jerusalem artichokes, leeks, mushrooms, pears, plums, potatoes, pumpkins/squash, quince, silverbeet/chard, turnips.

What to plant

Alfalfa, aloe vera, asparagus (seeds), azalea, bay tree, beetroot, bluebells, broad beans, broccoli, Brussels sprouts, Buxus, cabbage, calendula, carrots (best time), cauliflower, celeriac, chervil, chives, coriander/cilantro, Cosmos, cresses, daffodils, daisies, dill, English spinach, fennel, garden peas, garlic, garlic chives, globe artichokes, hyacinths, jonquils, lavender (seeds), leek, lemon, lettuce (best time), mint, mushroom kits, nasturtium, onions, pansies, parsley, parsnip, poppies, potatoes, radishes, silverbeet/chard, snow peas, spring onions/scallions, sugar snaps, tarragon, tulips, turnips, violas, Wollemi pine.

PART **3**

Baked pears

DIFFICULTY **1** MESS FACTOR **2** PREP TIME **15 MINS** COOKING TIME **20-25 MINS** FEEDS **4**

4 pears, peeled

160 ml water

1/3 cup runny honey

1 tsp ground cinnamon

Pears are a sensational autumn/fall fruit. Kids of all ages can make this recipe (little ones will appreciate your guidance). They can peel and place the pears on the foil, add the water, drizzle each pear with honey and sprinkle with cinnamon, and close the foil around the pears.

Method

Place each pear on a sheet of foil. Drizzle 2 tablespoons of water and 1 tablespoon of honey over each pear and sprinkle with cinnamon. Wrap loosely in foil.

Place the tray in the oven (or on the barbecue) to cook for 20–25 minutes or until tender. Serve with ice cream or custard.

seasons

Spring has sprung!

If you and your children are thinking of a spring bulb display, autumn is the time to buy most bulbs for storage and then planting. So visit your garden centre and choose a selection of bulbs.

If you have the space, try a mass planting of one particular bulb, such as daffodils, tulips or jonquils. If space is an issue, most bulbs will readily grow in a pot. Tulips look particularly pretty in a pot by the back door.

Follow the instructions on the bulb packet and your child is almost guaranteed a great display the following spring.

A reminder about the bulbs. To avoid disappointment, make sure your child plants the bulbs pointy side up! This rule applies to virtually all bulbs, but check with your local nursery if you are unsure. Don't forget, nearly every bulb, including members of the onion family, is toxic to the family dog.

Easy pumpkin soup

DIFFICULTY 2 | **MESS FACTOR 2** | **PREP TIME 15 MINS** | **COOKING TIME 35 MINS** | **FEEDS 4**

1 tbsp vegetable oil

1 brown onion, finely sliced

2 tsp finely chopped sage or rosemary leaves, half for the recipe, half for garnish

1 butternut pumpkin (squash), peeled and cubed

1 litre chicken stock

270 ml coconut milk (coconut milk is thin, coconut cream is thick)

Salt and pepper

Many pumpkins/squash are at their best in autumn/fall so encourage your children to try this yummy recipe. Your younger children can gather the ingredients from the fridge and pantry and pick the herbs from the garden. Children 7+ can have a try at making this by themselves.

Method

Heat the vegetable oil in a large saucepan over medium heat, add the onion and half the herbs and cook for 5 minutes or until soft.

Add the pumpkin and cook until golden on all sides. or you could roast the pumpkin instead as this intensifies the flavour.

Add the stock and coconut milk, bring to the boil, reduce heat to low and simmer for 20–25 minutes or until the pumpkin is soft. Season with salt and pepper. Blend for a smoother texture or leave as is if you like your soup chunky.

Garnish with the remaining herbs.

Decorating eggs for Easter

Now teenagers, and with their belief in the Easter Bunny waning, Easter egg hunts still remain a firm favourite with my children. We've been having simple hunts at our farm since they were tiny because it is such a joyous activity for both children and adults alike. Although the timing of when the eggs are hidden is now given more thought, as our resident fox has learned how to make off with his own haul of eggs. It's a wonder he hasn't killed himself because, as with dogs, chocolate is toxic to foxes.

If your children are under 6, keep the hunt a simple affair.

If your children are over 7, you could make an orienteering map complete with a series of riddles, to make them work a little harder to find their chocolate loot.

Easter is also a time when kids love making and giving homemade eggs as gifts. Hard-boil some eggs and let them cool. Using colouring-in pens, pencils, glitter or paint, have your younger children decorate them. Display them in a nest of feathers, sticks and other found objects, or give them to friends or family as a gift. (This type of Easter egg won't keep forever; we suggest you toss them after about a month.)

For older children 6+, you may wish to let them try their hand at blowing eggs (piercing the egg at both ends with a pin and blowing out the contents), but be prepared for a bit of a mess and a few smashed eggs. You can always use the contents for scrambled eggs. This style of Easter egg will keep forever, but is very fragile.

Curried/devilled eggs

DIFFICULTY 1 MESS FACTOR **3** PREP TIME **10 MINS** FEEDS **4-6**

8 fresh eggs

3–4 tbsp mayonnaise

1 tsp curry powder

½ tsp French mustard (optional)

½ tsp lemon juice

Salt and pepper

Curried eggs are simple to make and I've never known a child not to enjoy making and eating them. They are perfect for packing into your hamper for a picnic lunch (see page 46). Young children can help with the mixing of ingredients. Children 6+ can have a go at the entire recipe by themselves.

Method

Bring a large saucepan of water to the boil and gently place your eggs into the water. Cook for 6 minutes or until hard-boiled. Remove from the saucepan and allow to cool.

Meantime, put the mayonnaise, curry powder, mustard (optional), lemon juice and some salt and pepper into a bowl and mix to combine. Adjust to taste if necessary.

Gently peel the cooled eggs and cut in half. Scoop out the yolk and add to the mayonnaise mix. Stir well to combine. Again, adjust to taste if necessary.

Now scoop the egg/mayo mix back into the hollow of the egg where the yolk once was. Sprinkle with a little more curry powder or a pinch of paprika and serve. If you intend to take them on a picnic, place them in the fridge for half an hour or so until they have firmed up a little and are more easily transported in your hamper.

puddles of fun

Autumn/fall heralds the beginning of inclement weather – and with it, glorious puddles. No matter their age, children find them irresistible. After a shower of rain, go hunting for them and together with your children, jump, skip, squelch and splosh through all of them. Try it barefoot – there's nothing like it!

AUTUMNAL/FALL PHOTOGRAPHY

Choose a spot that you and your children can visit regularly and find a deciduous tree that is just starting to change colour. Take a camera and ask your children to take a really hard look at what is happening on the tree. They can then record it with a photo and add their observations into their journal.

Every other day, revisit the tree and try to take a photo from exactly the same spot. Compare the recordings. If you do this over the entire autumn/fall period, your child will be amazed by how much change has occurred over a short period of time. Once home, your children might like to print out their photos and make a visual calendar.

winter

Splash, shiver, snow, open fires, toasted marshmallows and winter skeletons. Winter is fun!

Winter is when the outdoors appears to go to sleep. Many plants and animals have bunkered down below the earth, waiting for the first touch of spring before reappearing.

It's a season of reflection: time to observe the bare bones of nature as magnificent deciduous trees show their 'winter skeletons'. There's cold, crisp weather and snow for many. Fires will be lit and marshmallows toasted. It's time to rug up and get outside!

In Winter I get up at night
And dress by yellow candle light.
In Summer, quite the other way,
I have to go to bed by day.

I have to go to bed and see
The birds still hopping on the tree,
Or hear the grown-up people's feet
Still going past me in the street.

And does it not seem hard to you,
When all the sky is clear and blue,
And I should like so much to play,
To have to go to bed by day?

Robert Louis Stevenson

PART 3

seasons

What to eat

Apples, Asian vegetables, broccoli, Brussels sprouts, cabbages, cauliflower, chervil, cumquats, fennel, leeks, lemons, lettuce, mandarins, navel oranges, parsnips, potatoes, rhubarb, silverbeet/chard, spinach, turnips.

What to plant

Aloe vera, apples, apricots, asparagus (bare-rooted), azaleas, bay tree, berries (most), Buxus, cherries, Chinese tallow tree, crepe myrtle, figs, fruit trees (most bare-rooted), grapes, hippeastrum, Jerusalem artichokes, lemon trees, mushroom kits, nectarines, peach, pear, plum, quince, rhubarb, roses (bare-rooted), Wollemi pines.

S·P·L·A·T·T·E·R PAINTING

Painting and writing in the snow with food colouring is such fun! Simply pour some food colouring or water-based craft paint into a squeezy bottle and start drawing in the snow. Lightly spraying water over the image creates an instant bleeding effect, which can look truly beautiful.

Suggest to your children that they photograph their artwork for posterity, as it won't last too long!

Lentil and vegetable minestrone

DIFFICULTY 1 MESS FACTOR **2** PREP TIME **10 MINS** COOKING TIME **40 MINS** FEEDS **6**

2 tbsp olive oil

2 leeks, white part only, finely sliced

1 large onion, finely chopped

2–3 garlic cloves, minced

1 tbsp finely chopped rosemary leaves (or whatever herbs you have in the garden)

Sprinkle of dried Italian herbs

Pinch of nutmeg

2 carrots, diced

½ red capsicum/bell pepper, diced

½ yellow capsicum/bell pepper, diced

2 celery stalks, finely chopped

3–4 ripe Roma tomatoes, finely chopped

400 g tin tomatoes, diced or crushed

1 handful of green beans, topped, tailed and chopped into 2 cm lengths

3 litres chicken stock

3 handfuls of red or green lentils

400 g tin cannellini beans

3 handfuls of your favourite short pasta (fusilli, penne or macaroni)

2 tbsp tomato paste

1 tbsp finely chopped flat leaf parsley, chives and basil for garnish.

Your young kids can collect the ingredients from the pantry or fridge and pick the herbs from the garden. Older children can get more involved.

Method

Heat the olive oil in a large saucepan over low heat. Add the leeks, onion, garlic, rosemary, dried herbs and nutmeg, then sweat, stirring occasionally, for 10 minutes or until the leek is soft and beginning to caramelise.

Add the carrots, capsicums, celery, tomatoes and green beans and cook for 5 minutes. Add the stock. Bring to a simmer, add the lentils and cannellini beans and simmer for 10–15 minutes. Throw in the pasta and cook for another 10 minutes. Stir in the tomato paste.

Spoon into soup bowls. Sprinkle with parsley, chives and basil and serve with toasted sourdough bread.

Simple can be best

Sometimes the simplest of activities can provide the most wonder.

When the weather permits, take a walk with your children in your local forest. You'll be amazed at what snow creatures you can see when you use your imagination. Spend time hunting for prints in the snow or mud and looking for fallen eggs, feathers and animal droppings. Take a small spade/shovel with you and hunt for buried treasure. Be sure to listen to the stillness that often accompanies a snowfall, along with the occasional groan of trees laden with snow and perhaps the hoot of a distant owl. Your children will be mesmerised.

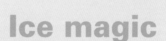

Ice magic

Suggest that your children head outdoors and find some small pretty objects from nature. Even in winter you can find oodles of treasure such as bright red berries from a holly bush, old rosehips, a few petals, tiny feathers, small funky-shaped leaves, discarded snail shells, etc.

Now fill an ice cube tray or cupcake baking tray with water and have your children place their objects into each hollow. Place in your refrigerator and freeze. Once completely frozen, turn out the cubes and cupcakes. Instant ice magic! The objects are trapped in the ice and can look truly beautiful when placed in natural light. They will sparkle and appear magnified. So pretty!

Have your children display them outside unless you want a series of small puddles in your living room within the hour! Again, taking photos of these masterpieces and sticking them into their journals is a must.

PART **3**

Snow art

A swathe of freshly fallen snow is like a giant white canvas. These natural canvases thrill children of all ages and are just begging to be decorated using objects found in nature. After rugging up, your children can head outside, collecting items such as large sticks, pine cones, pebbles and stones, fallen feathers – basically anything that grabs their fancy. Now encourage them to draw a square into the fresh snow and place these objects into their snowy canvas to create their own artistic masterpiece. They can also use the objects to create pretty imprints in the snow. And, of course, using their own body to create a snow angel is a must. Have a camera to hand to capture your children's artwork for all time.

Funky Faux Snowman

For those who don't have access to snow, here's a fun alternative. Put on some rubber gloves and then, with an electric mixer, beat white laundry powder with cold water. Add the water gradually to produce a gloopy mixture that holds together, is not runny, and can pack like a snowball.

Use this to help your children model a snowman. Add twigs or sticks for arms, berries or other found objects for eyes and a mouth, a small piece of material for a scarf (to keep him warm), a little bit off the end of a carrot for a nose, and a range of spiky sticks or gumnuts for a hat.

Sprinkle with clear, blue, silver or gold glitter for sparkle. Et voila! Mr Frosty, sans snow.

Toot, toot – out of my way! Even when our real roads are closed due to snow, our children can still go for a drive. Simply rug up, head outside and make a series of roads, on-ramps and off-ramps, using a shovel, in your front garden. Young children adore this activity and may spend hours pushing their diggers and cars around their make-believe highways. Encourage them to make some small snow bridges across the roads, with sticks for road signals. If they want to get really serious, they could make some signals using milk tops and Popsicle® sticks. Instant traffic jam!

seasons

Snowball Fights

Snowball fights are almost a rite of passage for children and I encourage them heartily. Just make sure you set out a few rules, such as no aiming at the head or close-up shots, and then let your kids at it! Their flushed, happy faces after racing about trying to perfect their shots are beautiful to behold. Sadly, many local authorities are now trying to ban snowball fights (Boo! Hiss!); if unsure, check with them before heading outdoors.

DANCING FLAMES There is nothing more magical and connecting than sitting around an open fire singing, sharing stories, creating music or simply appreciating the hypnotic dance and crackles of the flames. Even better when the weather is cold, but clear, and you are rugged up warmly. My children enjoy fires most at night during winter when the stars are also burning brightly.

Building a fire is a great physical activity for children of all ages. Once your fire is going well, why not bake some potatoes (wrapped in foil) or damper (see page 40) in the hot ashes, or toast some marshmallows on the end of long sticks until they are a toasted mass of sweet gooeyness.

Scarecrows and glittery bits

If you and your children have fruit trees or a vegetable garden of any size, building a scarecrow can help keep the birds at bay. Scale your scarecrow to fit your garden – the bigger the garden, the bigger the scarecrow.

Birds are clever creatures, though, and will eventually get used to your scarecrow. Your children might like to change his outfit and move him to a new place, so the birds will again be entirely unsure as to whether he's real or not!

If you don't have room for a scarecrow, attach foil, little bells or other shiny objects to smaller sticks or ice-cream lids and string and hang them over your precious vegetables or among your fruit trees.

You will need:

- a length of sturdy twine
- a hammer and a variety of nails
- two straight, sturdy branches (or pieces of wood), one approximately 2 m long, the other 1 m long
- an old basketball or other round ball for the head (a plastic bucket or small stuffed sack would also do)
- permanent markers

- old clothes for dressing the scarecrow
- an old pillow or cushion, or straw, sticks or shredded newspaper for stuffing and hair
- a sturdy stapler
- rubber gloves
- a selection of small bells
- waterproof string

Using some sturdy twine, or a large nail, secure the two branches or pieces of wood together to make a shape like a cross. Ask your children to draw a cranky looking face on the chosen head, and then you can make a hole in the bottom. If using a sack, stuff and secure with twine. Put to one side.

Now have your children dress the body of the scarecrow. Thread a shirt over his 'arms'. For a bit more authenticity, you can stuff him with an old pillow or cushion, straw or shredded newspaper. Pull some pants up over his 'leg' and secure all with twine or an old belt.

Once the children are happy with the scarecrow's wardrobe, help them stand him up and insert him firmly into the garden. Attach his head, put on a floppy hat and stuff some straw or sticks underneath for hair. Attach the hat with small nails, tacks or staples. Put the rubber gloves on the ends of the horizontal wood/stick to imitate hands and tack into place. Now stand back with your children and prepare to be scared!

Stuffed apples

DIFFICULTY 1 MESS FACTOR **2** PREP TIME **15 MINS** COOKING TIME **30 MINS** FEEDS **4-6**

150 g softened butter

½ cup soft brown sugar

1 tbsp sultanas

1 tbsp raisins

1 tsp ground cinnamon

Pinch of ground nutmeg

4–6 apples, cored

Kids of all ages can participate in making stuffed apples. They can make the mixture using their fingers, fill the apples with the mix and wrap them in foil.

Method

Preheat the oven to 180°C. Put the butter, brown sugar, sultanas, raisins, cinnamon and nutmeg in a bowl and combine.

Place each apple on a square of foil and spoon the mixture into the apple's cavity. Wrap the foil loosely around each apple to enclose.

Place apples on a baking tray, put in the oven or covered barbecue, and bake for 30 minutes or until soft. Serve with ice cream or custard.

PART 3

WINTER SKELETONS

During winter, the true outline or frames of deciduous trees are revealed in all their beauty. My children call them winter skeletons. When they were younger, they enjoyed spending time sitting outside sketching these trees and then adding their own leaves, using either colouring-in pens or the real leaves of evergreen trees, to create their own artwork.

This is a fun activity for children of all ages. Instead of encouraging them to use traditional tree colours if colouring in, suggest using rainbow or fluorescent colours, glitter glue or funky shaped stickers. Their imagination will amaze you.

While they are sketching, talk to them about how, by observing the winter frame of a deciduous tree, they can perhaps picture the hidden roots of the tree. Did you know that, overall, roots mirror almost exactly the shape of its branches? That is, what you see on top, you'll find below!

Ocean Watch

With over 70 per cent of the earth covered in water of some form, oceans are a fascinating and ever-changing natural wonder. From the brilliant blues and greens of every shade on a fine day to the greys, white foamy caps, purples and murky greens on stormy days, the colour of the ocean is never the same, particularly in winter. This provides young children with a completely different perspective on the colours of Mother Nature, as well as an understanding of the power of the ocean.

From the ocean also come many interesting treasures that have been blown onto the shore: driftwood, seaweed, larger shells – maybe even a message in a bottle!

seasons

Senses

Touch

Taste

Sight

Smell

Sound

The senses of our children come into their own when they step outside the front door. Whether it's picking and eating a tomato straight off the plant, smelling the pavement after a downpour, feeling the touch of summer sun on their back, watching a caterpillar inch its way along a leaf or listening to the many sounds of nature, each one has its own place in developing an understanding and lasting love of the outdoors.

touch

Crinkly, prickly, soft, velvety, slimy, cold, warm, spiky, fluffy. Give your child access to the 'feel' of the outside and they are bound to come up with their own words to describe what they find.

SCULPTURAL MASTERPIECES

You never know, the next Michelangelo might be lurking in your home. To find out, buy some modelling clay, put on art smocks and choose a place outside. Working with clay is not as messy as the mud version (see page 100) and allows little fingers to become more dexterous and to create more detailed works of art. This in turn helps with imagination, creativity and concentration. The masterpieces can be baked in a cool oven and then painted using non-toxic acrylic paints.

Mystery collection

Take a walk with your children around your garden and neighbourhood and collect as many varied objects as you can, such as flowers, shells, seaweed, bark, a conker, a fallen bird's egg, a gumnut, a couple of 'smelly' herbs, some stones or pebbles, a soft-spined cactus or succulent, some feathers. It may take several outings until your children are satisfied with their collection.

A day or so later, when some of the items have been forgotten, arrange the selection in a flat box. A shoebox with a hand-sized hole cut in the lid is a good option. At the last minute, add an ice cube.

Now, encourage your child or children to feel around inside the box without looking (use a blindfold if necessary) and withdraw one item. They must guess what it is from its touch and smell. Repeat the activity.

Once finished, ask your children to bunch similar objects together and make a permanent display that can be added to over time. They can also do drawings of their found items if they wish. This activity is best suited to children 6+.

the perfect mud pie

Most children love slurpy, gooey, squelchy mud. Its texture, feel and (sometimes) taste are irresistible. Think of it as the outdoor equivalent of play dough.

Choose a sunny day and be prepared for a big mess. The best part of this activity is that your children can do every aspect of it, including collecting the equipment, and together you can wash it all back into the garden when you are finished.

You will need:

- soil
- a small bucket
- a coarse sieve or colander
- containers of different sizes
- water
- a small watering can
- a few spoons, scoops, or small plastic spades
- a flat tray, or some large squares of aluminium foil or flat pieces of thick cardboard
- washable art smocks (optional)
- found objects for decorating – feathers, flowers, small sticks, pebbles, etc.

Together, go hunting for soil – a bucketful should do the trick. Have your child pour the soil through the sieve removing any large objects as they go. If the objects are interesting, encourage them to add them to their found object collection (see previous page). Ask them to return any wriggly worms they find to the garden.

Divide the soil into containers so each child has an equal amount. Slowly add some water until it forms a gooey consistency. Too much water and you'll need to add more soil. A soil with a heavy clay content will hold its shape better than a sandy soil. You can add some plain flour to your soil if need be. Let the children squish it between their fingers, pound it, roll it and make any shape they wish. Hits with my children have included mud pies in the shape of a cake, dog poo, small balls, worms or snakes, sticks and mud snowmen. Place the finished products on a flat tray, decorate with some found objects and leave to 'bake' in the sun until completely dry.

Playing in the mud doesn't need to be as structured as this. Simply running and sliding through it, sploshing about in it and squelching it through their fingers are wonderful sensory experiences for little ones. Some children have a real aversion to messy activities, so you might consider using plasticine or modelling clay instead of mud if this is the case.

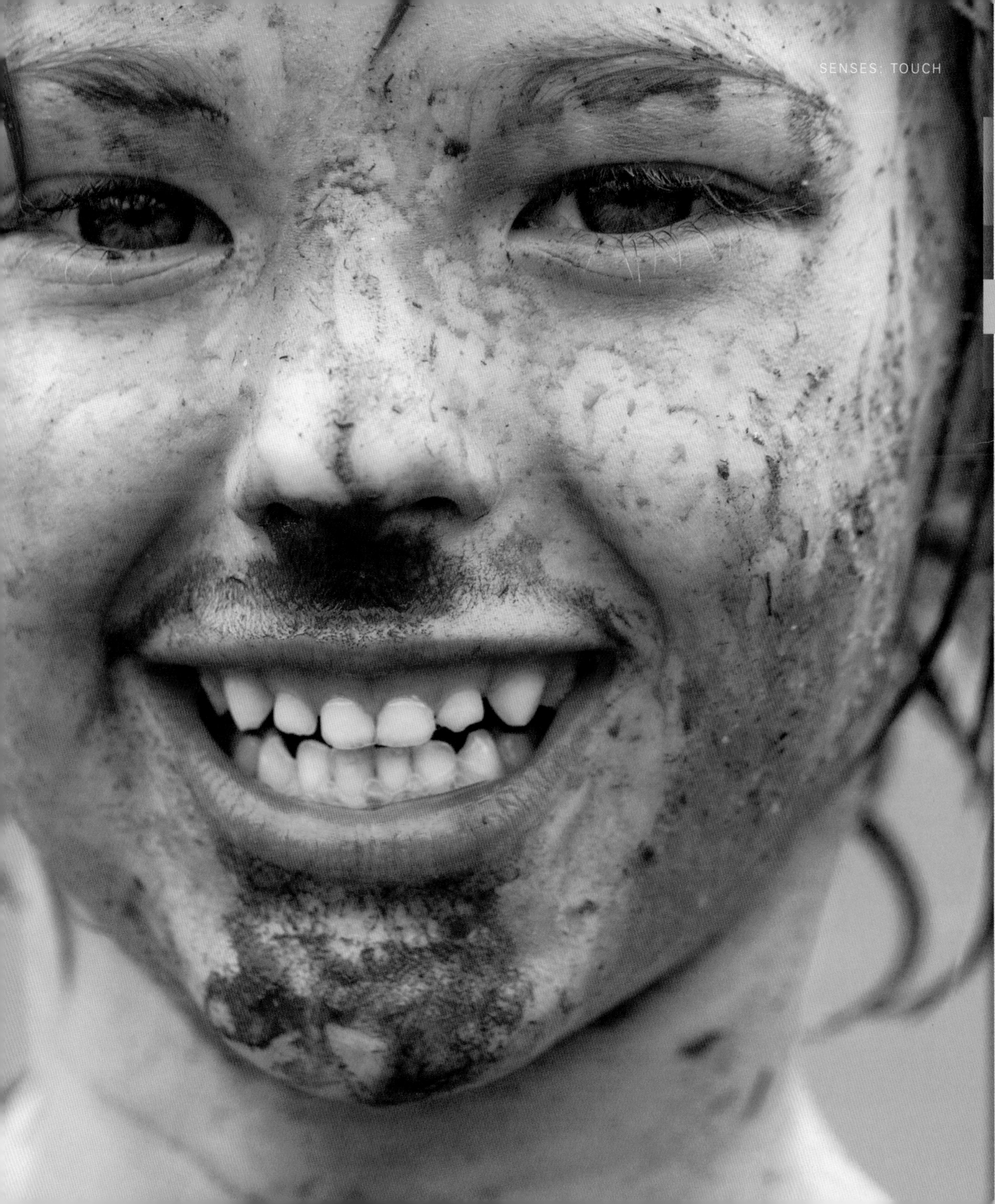

Simple play with rain

Wait for a warm but rainy day. Put on raincoats (or if it's really warm, ask your children if they want to go naked – some children can be shy) and encourage them to go outside and catch the rain on their tongues. They will love the sensation of the rain on their face and they may concentrate really hard and stay still for quite a while, trying to experience the touch and taste of those elusive drops.

Blind man's bluff

This fun and simple activity can be played with as many children (and adults) as you wish in a spacious and preferably enclosed area. Younger children may not enjoy having their eyes covered, so be guided by your child's preference.

One of the players is nominated 'it', and a blindfold (an airline eye mask or large handkerchief is ideal) is put over his/her eyes. 'It' then has to grope about, trying to find the other players by touch. If the game is being played by older children, the players can move about to try and avoid 'It'. For little ones this is a more satisfying game if the other players select a position and stand still. As each player is found, they leave the game, until only one person is left. When 'It' finds them, they must touch their face and try to guess who it is.

The game should be played on a level, preferably grassed area that has been cleared of any objects over which children could trip and hurt themselves. This includes the family pet!

Marco Polo

A version best suited to slightly older children and those who are confident in water is a game called Marco Polo. Played in a swimming pool or at the beach (without a blindfold, but with closed eyes, except when under water – I've never known a child who can actually resist the temptation to open their eyes!) – 'It' calls out, 'Marco'. The other players respond with 'Polo' until everyone has been found by touch.

Prickly bits

Cacti and succulents are remarkable plants. They require little care or water and love being in full sun (either inside or out), so they can be looked after easily by children of all ages. They are available in lots of different shapes and sizes. Some are very thorny, some almost feathery in appearance and some produce the most beautiful flowers.

Take a trip to your garden centre and encourage your children to select three or four different types of cacti and succulents. Be guided by the centre as to the most appropriate species for young children.

At home, find an old container or plastic toy truck that has seen better days. You'll need to make drainage holes in the bottom. Fill the container with some sandy potting mix (observe the safety instructions on the bag) and plant away.

Encourage your children to feel the prickles as they go. They will very quickly learn to be deft with their touch. Ask your child to think up a name for each plant, write it on a small piece of paper and attach it to the plant. Instant cactus personality!

If you are not keen on the thought of cacti, why not consider the beautiful and very useful aloe vera plant or other succulent? Virtually indestructible, it has similar habits to cacti and the sap of the plant can be used to soothe bites and stings and assist in the relief of dry skin.

taste

We all love tasting things. It is one of the most used senses by very little children. They will pop nearly anything – or everything – into their mouths. The experience of biting into a crunchy sweet apple, munching on a herb picked straight from the garden or simply tasting something new for the very first time can create memories that last a lifetime.

PART 4

FLORAL CUBES

With your child, collect a dozen or so viola or pansy flowers and wash them gently. Pop them into an ice cube tray and fill with water. Freeze.

Tip frozen cubes into a glass and fill with your child's favourite drink (see page 45 for a homemade cordial recipe).

Every part of the flower is edible, but the petals have the mildest flavour. You can also use these flowers to jazz up salads, and they press beautifully too.

senses

One for the pets

If you own a cat or a dog, you might like to consider having your child plant some of the following herbs in your garden. Catnip, Catmint and Cat Grass are irresistible to – you guessed it – cats. Pennyroyal is considered a flea deterrent by some. You might like to plant some near your dog's kennel as a natural way of keeping fleas at bay. On the other hand, if you want to keep dogs out of the garden, try Dogbane. It's aptly named – they hate the stuff. And chooks just love Chickweed, which is great because it's a real pest in lawns and garden beds.

Caro's Goddess sauce

DIFFICULTY 1 | MESS FACTOR 2 | PREP TIME 20 MINS | MAKES 3 SMALL JARS

2 cups of a combination of green herbs such as parsley, tarragon, chervil, chopped roughly

3 eschallots, peeled

2 large cloves of garlic, peeled

Juice of 2 lemons

1 large piece lemon rind (no pith)

½ tsp chilli flakes (optional)

2 tsp sea salt or kosher salt

1 tsp freshly ground black pepper

1 cup quality egg mayonnaise

4 anchovy fillets

1 cup quality sour cream or crème fraîche

This is a great recipe for children 7+ to add to their cooking armoury and its history will also interest them. Legend has it that Chef Philip Roemer first made it in 1923 at the Palace Hotel in San Francisco. He wanted to pay tribute to the actor George Arliss and his hit play, The Green Goddess. However, it is simply a variation of Sauce au Vert (Green Sauce), which initially appeared at the court of Louis XIII. Then, apparently, the sauce was served with green eel – euk!

Wherever it originated, it is simply the most delicious sauce or dressing. It goes with just about everything and is super easy to make. Encourage your child to have a go at making it. You may well find it becomes a staple in your fridge where it will keep for up to a week.

Method

Roughly chop all the ingredients, and then put into a blender and whiz until well combined and a fine, creamy texture is achieved. This shouldn't take more than a few minutes at most. You might need to do this in batches depending on how big your blender is. If this is the case, once you've done so, give the entire batch a final stir in a large bowl at the end so the flavour is distributed evenly. Adjust seasoning to taste.

The original recipe doesn't use lemon zest or chilli, but I think they add further zing. When choosing your herbs, simply select those you most prefer. A more traditional green sauce? Chervil, tarragon and parsley are best. A bit of an Asian twist? Coriander/cilantro, basil, mint, Vietnamese mint and garlic chives could be used. Just experiment and have fun!

Lavender scoops

Collect some culinary lavender flowers with your child. Cut off the stems and have your child gently shred the flowers. Put some ice cream in a cone, drizzle a little honey on top and sprinkle with a few lavender flowers. Return outdoors and eat. Yum! The flowers of this remarkable plant can also be used in drinks and cakes.

Some lavenders are not pleasant to eat. Only culinary lavender should be used . English (*Lavendula angustifolia*) and French lavender is fine (English is better); Italian and Spanish lavender is best suited to other purposes. (See pages 120, 121 and 123 for other activities using lavender.)

Rocket/arugula pesto

DIFFICULTY **1** MESS FACTOR **2** PREP TIME **10 MINS** FEEDS **4-6**

2 cups rocket/arugula leaves, stalks removed

2–3 garlic cloves, peeled and chopped

1½ cups grated Parmesan cheese

¼ cup toasted pine nuts

1 cup olive oil

Salt and pepper

Juice of half a lemon

Your child can collect all the ingredients and pick the rocket, and then remove the leaves from the stalk and help measure the ingredients. They can also place all the ingredients in the blender. Children 6+ can make this dish on their own. Pesto can be eaten with crackers as a dip or mixed through cooked pasta for a simple, tasty dinner. If you don't have any rocket/arugula to hand, you can substitute basil leaves.

Method

Place rocket, garlic, Parmesan and pine nuts in a food processor and whiz until it forms a paste. With the motor running, add the olive oil in a thin, steady stream and process until the mixture is smooth and takes on a slightly creamy appearance. Add salt and pepper and lemon to taste and more olive oil if a thinner consistency is required.

Stuffed zucchini/courgette flowers

DIFFICULTY 4 MESS FACTOR **5** PREP TIME **20 MINS** COOKING TIME **5 MINS** FEEDS **3-4**

8–10 zucchini/courgette flowers

20 tbsp of fresh ricotta

Zest of 1 lemon

Small handful of shredded fresh basil or a few teaspoons of fresh lemon thyme

Handful of pine nuts, toasted

Tiny squeeze of honey

Salt and pepper

2 egg whites, lightly beaten

Plain flour for dusting

Vegetable oil for frying

This recipe can be a bit fiddly so be prepared for a bit of mess.

Method

Begin by gently prising the petals of the flower apart and removing the yellow stamens in the centre of the flower. This is a good activity for little fingers as it assists with developing fine motor control. You will need to help very little children with this step. You can leave the stamens in if need be, but they can be a bit bitter.

Set the flowers aside. Put the ricotta, lemon zest, herbs, pine nuts, honey and a crack of salt and pepper into a mixing bowl and stir until well combined. Taste and adjust if necessary. The mix should taste quite savoury with just a hint of sweetness from the honey. Now spoon the mix into the cavity of your flowers. Twist the end of the petals gently to prevent the mix escaping.

Brush the flowers with the egg whites and then roll in plain flour until lightly dusted. You can complicate this step by making a proper tempura batter, but I've never had the patience to do that!

Heat some vegetable oil in a deep fry pan and gently shallow fry the flowers in batches until golden (about 5 minutes). Serve with a few grilled lamb chops – and eat the lot! Delicious!

My promise to you is that I've never known a child who can resist eating zucchini/courgette flowers.

Instant herb box

Visit a garden centre and let your child choose some potted herbs. When selecting them, try to group those herbs together that like similar growing conditions. Most herbs like full sun, but some do better in partial shade.

Back home, plant the herbs evenly in a large pot or wooden box. Use a premium potting mix and water them well. After the herbs have grown for a while, say two weeks, you can begin the activity.

For fun, blindfold your child and ask them to taste each one. They can then choose a favourite and together you can cook something using that herb. (Older children might like being blindfolded, while children under three most often prefer to see what they're touching.)

If a herb garden is not feasible, you and your children can still do this activity using bunches of herbs found at most supermarkets and greengrocers.

Less common herbs you might want to try include sage, chervil, garlic chives, Vietnamese mint, Holy basil, tarragon and lemon verbena.

Remember that for very young children taste is one of the most used senses. Everything goes into the mouth and this can include some truly horrible and potentially poisonous things that may be scooped up when outside. Be watchful and start lessons early about what's edible and what's not.

senses

THE HUMBLE HERB

Basil – at its best in the summer months. There are various forms of basil available – keep an eye out for the purple, curly and lime-coloured varieties. Easy to grow, with a variety of uses, basil is great with tomatoes, cheeses and olives, chicken dishes and can be used as a garnish on pizzas.

Chives – will grow just about anywhere. With a mild flavour, compared to onion and garlic, they are a good introduction to the onion family for children. Delicious with fish or potatoes, in salads and sprinkled over freshly sliced tomatoes, they are also perfect for decorating dishes when kids are helping in the kitchen.

Coriander/cilantro – a polarising herb. Some adore it, others loathe it. Regardless, it is relatively easy to grow, has a strong, unique flavour that my children took a while to get used to, but now love, adding it to many of the Asian dishes we prepare.

Dill – a lovely herb, with a delightful feathery appearance. Dill is easy to grow, but will get quite tall if left to its own devices, so space might be an issue. It's perfect with fish. Some people say dill is a cure for hiccups, so if you have a regular hiccuper in the household, have them nibble a bit whenever the hiccups strike unexpectedly.

Mint – a cheeky, fast-growing herb, often out-competing other plants for space in the garden. Because of this, it is preferable to grow it in its own pot. It is delicious chopped and sprinkled over peas and potatoes and in salads. It also makes a refreshing cup of tea. Try chopping up some pineapple, strawberries, melon and mangoes, threading them onto wooden skewers and interspersing the fruit with mint leaves. Other common forms of mint include spearmint,

peppermint and applemint. Chocolate mint sprinkled over fresh strawberries and chocolate ice cream is delicious.

Oregano – like thyme is fast growing and spreading in habit. It is delicious when added to most tomato-based dishes and adds oomph to chicken too. If making pizzas with faces, have the children use it to add some hair.

Parsley – the most common forms are continental/Italian flat-leaf parsley and curly parsley. The continental version has a slightly milder taste. Parsley can be added to just about any meal prepared for children. Here's an idea I like. Prepare some soft-boiled eggs for breakfast or lunch, along with some crunchy wholemeal toast. When the eggs have cooled, ask your children to draw a face on the eggshells. Then slice off the top and add some curly parsley – instant hairy egg man!

Rocket/arugula – a perfect herb for young children to grow. It's almost foolproof and aptly named because it shoots up from seed or seedling very fast. Children love watching it grow and should be able to eat their first leaf within 2–4 weeks.

Rosemary – a beautiful perennial herb that can be used for all sorts of culinary purposes. It forms the herb base of many casseroles, soups and pasta dishes and is great infused into oil. You might like to consider making some with your children.

Thyme – a relatively fast-growing and spreading herb. Delicious with chicken dishes, it can be grown in a pot by the back door. Consider trying lemon thyme for its tangy taste. You can add it to children's omelettes or, if you and your children like baking bread, add it to the dough to make yummy, lemony bread.

There are literally thousands of different herbs. Since the beginning of human existence, they have been used for culinary, medicinal and, in some cases, spiritual purposes. You've got to love them if only for their adaptability. Fresh or dry, they add zing to your child's food and give them an appreciation of the variety of tastes offered by Mother Nature.

I've chosen 10 that can be planted, tended and harvested easily by young children. You can find them at garden centres in seed, seedling or plant form. If you don't have any planting space, you can also find them as cut bunches at supermarkets and greengrocers.

senses

Edible flowers

Did you know that the flowers of many herbs and other flowering plants are edible? They can really spice up a salad or casserole, and children love looking for the perfect flower to make pretty drinks on a hot summer's day.

It is vital, however, that lessons on what is edible and what is not start early. Children should never eat anything from the plant world unless they first check with you. Put simply, if you are unsure, don't eat it. Always ask which parts of a herb or other plant are edible at the point of purchase. For example, the stems of rhubarb are edible but its leaves are poisonous. In fact, many plants commonly found in gardens and parks are poisonous. Make sure also that you only eat flowers that haven't been sprayed with chemicals.

Flowers of each of the following plants are edible and all of these plants are easy for children to plant, tend and harvest. They can also be grown in a pot if your outdoor space is limited.

Basil – has small pretty white or purple flowers that can be used in salads or as a garnish on frittatas, pizzas and quiches.

Borage – one of the prettiest of the flowering herbs. The flowers can be used in salads, dips and as a general garnish. They can be put into ice cubes (like violas and pansies) and they can be sugared for use as cake decoration. They are also great in potpourri. Don't go overboard with your use of borage.

Broccoli – will flower if let go. You and your children may have already noticed this if you have planted it in your garden in the past. The flowers are small and bright yellow and, not surprisingly, taste of broccoli. For many, the challenge of getting young children to eat broccoli can be almost insurmountable. Faced with this when my children were very little, I gave up on the floret and instead started sprinkling small amounts of broccoli flowers on top of whatever we had prepared for dinner. It made the meal look interesting and became irresistible to my children. As teens, they now inhale broccoli with relish! Both the florets and the flowers can be added to salads and stir-fries.

Chives – produce a very pretty purple flower that looks a bit like a small pom-pom. With its mild onion flavour, chive flowers can be sprinkled over vegetables or added to salads.

Marigolds – comes in a range of sunny colours and brighten up any meal. The petals can be used in salads or sprinkled over rice, pizzas, pasta and soups. The taste can be a bit spicy for young ones, so introduce them sparingly.

Marjoram, oregano and thyme – these flowers make a perfect garnish for frittatas, pizzas and quiches and can also be added to lamb, chicken and fish dishes.

Nasturtium – these flowers are crammed with vitamin C. They can be eaten whole, or used in salads or as a garnish. The leaves are also edible but best served sliced finely. They have a delicious sweet and slightly spicy flavour.

Pumpkin and zucchini/courgette – unbeatable for taste, ease of growing and their brilliant visual display. Harvest the flowers and baby zucchini in spring and eat the lot! (See recipe on page 108.)

Rose – petals are edible, but the flavour depends on the type and colour of the bloom. They look beautiful sprinkled over desserts and salads and can also be used in jellies and syrups and sugared for cake decoration. Rose petals look gorgeous bobbing about in the bath with young children and add a delicious fragrance to the water, too. See page 121 for another activity using rose petals.

Rosemary – has very dainty flowers that can be used in casseroles and soups and as a garnish on meat. They can also be used when baking breads and damper and in jellies and syrups. You can create skewers for meats or vegetables by cutting a stem (around 15 cm in length), stripping the foliage and leaving a small bunch of the flowers at the tip. Not only are these fun for kids to make (assisting with fine motor skills is a bonus), whatever you are cooking will take on a lovely rosemary flavour.

Sage – these flowers are perfect for using in soups and casseroles and as a garnish. They are quite delicious when pan fried in butter with a few sage leaves until they become crispy. They can also be used in stuffing. There are many varieties of sage, some of which are not appropriate for eating, so choose with care. The bright red flowers of the fragrant pineapple sage are delicious sprinkled over fresh pineapple or ice cream, or used as a garnish on an iced butter cake.

senses

sight

The outdoors is a magical place for little eyes. There are real and imagined things to be seen everywhere. Encourage your children to look up, down and all around – and delight in watching them take it all in.

SUNFLOWERS

Of all the flowers a child can grow, the sunflower is the most joyous, with its large happy face that follows the sun while growing. Little ones can almost see it inching its way up, up, up!

Sunflowers come in many varieties and colours and some can grow to 8 m, so make sure you help your child choose one to suit your garden. There are smaller varieties that are suitable for pots.

All each of them asks is for plenty of sun, a bit of love and some water. Follow the instructions on the seed packet and your child is almost certain to be rewarded.

Once the seeds have dried on the plant, your children can harvest them. They can be eaten raw or toasted (make sure you remove the outer husk before eating) – or saved for future plantings.

LOOKING UP

At the local park, beach or on the expanse of a rural property, kites can be the perfect way to while away a sunny, breezy afternoon. Young children – especially those who are at the stage of wanting to do everything by themselves – find flying kites tremendously challenging and rewarding. They are also great fun for older children to make.

If you do decide to go kite flying, make sure your kite is sturdy, but lightweight, and pretty much guaranteed to fly in the vaguest of breezes. This will help avoid frustration setting in as the inevitable crashes occur and will enable the really little ones to have a go at holding the kite by themselves. Remember, power lines can kill: look up and always encourage your children to do the same before flying their kite.

senses

Night walk

As confidence and independence increases in children, they will adore going on a night walk with you.

Listen out for frogs and other sounds of the night including the growl of a neighbour's dog (or was that a dragon?), a car passing by, a sudden rustle in the branches, and look for fairies fluttering home after a busy day. By mixing the real with the imagined, your child will be mesmerised.

For those who might be genuinely scared of the dark, follow a path that you walk regularly during daylight hours, pointing out as you go that everything is as it was; it's just harder to see, that's all.

Super sleuth

Encourage your children to head outdoors with their very own homemade magnifying glass to see what they can find!

All you need do is purchase a pair of reading glasses from your local pharmacy, bookstore or supermarket. They aren't generally very expensive as the lenses within them aren't prescription, just simple bits of magnified glass. They come in a range of 'strengths'. Choose glasses with the highest level of magnification and, when home, you'll find you can pop out the glass from the frames quite easily. Now get a icy pole stick and help your child attach it firmly to one of the pieces of glass using sticky tape. Et voilà! You now have an instant magnifying glass for your young child.

It can be fun to dress up like a super sleuth and together go looking for things in nature that benefit from a 'micro' look. Flowers, insects, small stones, shells and a patch of soil all look completely different when viewed close-up and will fascinate your child.

Up and down

Sunrises and sunsets can be spectacularly beautiful. Every now and then, find a place where together you can watch the sun come up or set. Point out how the sun starts low, goes up, up, up and then down, down, down. Simple as that, but something children will enjoy tremendously and remember.

The moon, or Luna, as she's called in our home, fascinates children. Some may associate her with going to bed; others may daydream about flying to her. Many will firmly believe she is made of cheese. At their own speed, they will come to realise that she rises and sets just like the sun. On a clear night, why not consider going moon watching just before bed?

Young children are intrigued by how one day she is a perfect ball and on another day a tiny shining crescent, and why sometimes she looks enormous sitting on the horizon and soon 'shrinks' to a small ball. I know I struggled with explaining the waxing and waning of the moon to my children when they were little, but I soon realised that quite honestly they didn't need such a detailed explanation. However, children 8+ might want to do a little research on why that is. You could also encourage them to start a moon journal so they can track its process over a month or even a year.

Lunar eclipses are another fascinating phenomenon for young children to experience.

senses

Catch that insect!

Insects of all kinds fascinate young ones but some children might be fearful, so be guided by your knowledge of your child before undertaking this activity. Obviously some insects are best left alone, so in this case be guided by your knowledge of insects when helping your children catch and care for creepy-crawlies.

You will need:

- a shoebox or other small cardboard box
- some grass, sticks, soil and a few flowers
- a couple of sheets of clear cellophane or plastic wrap
- large rubber band, sticky tape or light masking tape
- two empty toilet rolls
- a magnifying glass (see page 116 for homemade version) some cotton wool balls.

Have your children imagine what insects they might catch and ask them to draw them around the outside of the box. Put a few sticks, a bit of grass, some soil and a flower or two in the box. Help them cover the top of the box with clear cellophane or plastic wrap, piercing it here and there as you go to provide a few air holes. (Keep them small unless you want escapees!) Attach this securely to the box with a large rubber band, some sticky tape or light masking tape.

Make a larger hole in the cover and gently insert one of the empty toilet rolls. Secure it using sticky tape. This is to funnel the insects into their new home.

Your children are now ready to set off exploring. Using their magnifying glass, they will probably be able to locate a good selection of insects. They can use their second toilet roll to scoop them up and then tip them through the first toilet roll and straight into the box. Once your children are satisfied with their collection, secure the funnel by stuffing it with cotton wool balls. Encourage your children to release their catch every few days and replace with new insects.

smell

Smell is one of the most evocative of the senses. When I smell the sweet scent of Daphne, I am instantly transported to my Grandmother's house. The perfume of Corymbia citriodora or Lemon Scented Gum whisks me straight to the sub-tropical forests of southern Australia. My children refer to smell as the instant memory-maker. The outdoors is jam-packed with amazing and diverse smells. From the delicious to the downright disgusting, there's something for everyone!

FLOWER POWER

When I was young, my mother used to drag me out of bed at a ridiculously early hour to visit the flower markets. I disliked intensely the sleepy trip in half-darkness, but that was forgotten the instant we stepped inside the vast hall overflowing with a million flowers of every shape and scent.

It has become a memory that I treasure, so I can recommend the pain of waking a sleeping child at 4 am every so often. It is an overwhelming sensory experience for young children and you can pick up some beautiful blooms cheaply, too.

senses

On the nose   Together, take a walk around your neighbourhood and collect a variety of objects with different smells, such as flowers and blossoms, leaves (many will release a delicious, or truly awful, smell when gently crushed), bark, berries, seeds, seaweed, sea shells, empty snail shells, grasses or pebbles. Encourage your children to sniff while they walk. They might catch the whiff of an overstuffed garbage bin, some dog poo, the smell of a dead animal (yuk), a burst of roses hanging over a fence, someone's lunch cooking, the smell of a car backfiring, or the delicious smell in the air after a shower of rain. (Did you know that the latter has its very own name? It's called Petrichor).

Once you are home, have them arrange their objects and take turns to describe the smell of each one – is it sweet, bitter, spicy, salty, earthy, or just downright disgusting? This encourages children to think of new descriptive words and phrases. Watch for little ones trying to taste their objects!

Stinky pup!   Owning a pet brings a set of responsibilities that young children, on the whole, don't fully appreciate. The most unpleasant thing about owning a dog is the need to regularly scoop up their poo. Young children will be fascinated by it, but for obvious reasons will not want to have anything to do with it. So it makes sense, given your family pet will be with you for about 10 years, that lessons about cleaning up after your dog need to start early. When the time is right, encourage your child to help with cleaning up using a large, long-handled scoop. In fact, it is a good regular chore to give your older children. And remember to pack some poop bags when setting out for a walk with your dog. It goes without saying that good hygiene must be observed at all times when cleaning up after a dog.

To maintain a healthy pack order in your family, children should also be given the job of feeding the family pet because, to the dog's mind, whoever feeds them is definitely above them in the pecking order.

I don't know why my children thought of adding coloured pencil shavings to their rose petal potpourri, but I'm glad they did. To make the potpourri, you will need:

- 6–8 large handfuls (20 little handfuls) of fresh, colourful and perfumed rose petals
- some rose leaves
- a handful of tiny rosebuds (optional)
- 1 large handful of shredded lavender flowers
- a couple of pencil sharpeners.
- a selection of coloured pencils
- 1–2 tsp of orris root powder
- 10–12 drops of rose oil

With your child, collect the roses and lavender. Roses generally bloom in late spring, throughout summer and sometimes have a late autumn/fall flush. Lavender is at its most prolific in summer.

Place the rose petals, leaves and lavender on a cooling rack and leave in an airy spot until dry (this should take about a week). It's a good idea to move them about on the tray each day. You can dry rosebuds in the same way.

Ask your children to sharpen their coloured pencils and place the shavings in a bowl. Combine with the rest of the dry ingredients.

Gently transfer the mixture into a large paper bag, add the orris root powder, hold the bag closed and carefully toss the ingredients so the powder is evenly distributed. You really should store this bag away for a month or so, but little ones will struggle with waiting so long.

When you're ready, tip the contents of the paper bag back into your bowl and sprinkle with drops of rose oil. You may need to add a few more drops every six months or so.

Rose petal and pencil shaving potpourri

senses

TUSSIE MUSSIES

Way back in the days when the smells of urban living could be abhorrent and plague was a threat, people used to make these simple little posies, using fresh herbs and other common flowering plants, to give to others or to hold under their nose when venturing out.

My children love making and giving tussie mussies, as an unexpected gift to Grandma, special friends and every now and then their teachers. By using the herbs you have to hand (those with woody stems are easier to arrange), your children can make a sweet-smelling and relatively long-lasting arrangement.

You will need:

- long sprigs of rosemary
- long stems of lavender
- long sprigs of a bay, lime, lemon or orange tree (even better if flowering)
- long sprigs of sage (even better if it's flowering)
- long stems of mint (any kind will do)
- long stems of curly parsley
- long stems of tea roses
- a rubber band
- some decorative string or ribbon
- gift tags

Together, combine the flowers and herbs to make a small posy. Have your children write and attach a little note of good wishes and watch as they win the heart of the recipient.

Easy lavender bags

The smell of lavender is calming, and when placed under a child's pillow at night is said to assist restful sleep.

You will need one piece of fabric 25 cm long by 8 cm wide (or bigger if you want). Simply fold in half and sew down both sides. With your child, find enough lavender flowers to fill the bag (they are at their best in summer). To dry the lavender, separate the stems as much as possible and place on a cake rack. Put in an airy room for around two weeks or until the lavender becomes crisp to the touch. If space is limited, tie the lavender into a loose bunch and hang in an airy spot, blooms facing down. When the lavender is completely dry, gently shred the flowers off the top of the stems, sprinkle with a little lavender oil and scoop into the bag. Sew it up and tie with ribbon. Place under your child's pillow and enjoy a good night's sleep!

Gumnut potpourri

This potpourri reminds my children of Christmas, either because of the spicy smell of the cloves mixed with orange or the sweet cinnamon smell so my kids and I generally make it towards the end of the year. You might also wish to buy some cellophane bags, into which you can put the potpourri, to give as Christmas gifts.

You will need:

- handful of orange leaves (and, if possible, orange flowers)
- 1 firm orange
- 1–2 tsp of orris root powder
- a few cinnamon quills
- a handful of cloves
- a selection of dried gumnuts (or interesting seed pods)
- drops of orange blossom oil
- drops of cinnamon oil.

Dry the orange leaves and flowers on a cake rack in a light, airy spot for a week or so or until crisp to the touch. Slice the orange into thin rings around 5 mm in width. Rub with some of the orris root powder. Place on a cake tray in a cool oven (120°C) until the orange has dried and become crisp without burning. Remove and cool completely.

In a decorative bowl of your child's choice, combine the cinnamon quills, cloves, gumnuts and dried orange leaves, flowers and segments. Now gently transfer the mixture into a large paper bag and add the remainder of the orris root powder. Hold the bag closed and gently toss the ingredients so the orris root is distributed evenly. Again, you really should store this bag away for a month or so, but we've never had the patience for that. Empty the contents of the paper bag back into your bowl and sprinkle with a few drops of each of the essential oils. Every month or so, you might need to add a few more drops of oil.

senses

sound

The outdoors is the perfect place to let children be as noisy as they wish. Let them yell, laugh, sing and scream their little hearts out! However, it's also a place of reflection where together you can kick off your shoes, lie under a tree and quietly listen to the amazing sounds of your local environment.

wind chimes

Children adore the sound of wind chimes tinkling on a breezy day. Most adults do too! Here's an idea for some chimes you can make at home and hang outside. Given the need for an adult to pierce holes in objects, you may find that your younger child will be more of an assistant on this project, but they'll still get a buzz out of it.

You will need:

- a small plastic jelly mould or other decorative container
- a small screwdriver or other implement for piercing holes in plastic
- a hammer (optional)
- sturdy fishing line that can be knotted
- four or five small (rustproof) metal nuts
- decorative plastic buttons and large beads with holes
- four or five old heavy-duty plastic spoons, forks or other kitchen utensils
- a small rustproof hook.

Pierce a small hole in the centre of the mould and pass the fishing line through it so that half the line is protruding from the top and half from the bottom.

Thread a metal nut onto the line (on the inside of the mould) and tie a large, sturdy knot halfway along the line so the line can no longer slip through. The nut will stop this happening.

Thread and tie several large, heavy buttons or beads onto the bottom bit of the line. This is the central piece of the chime.

Meanwhile, ask your child to select a variety of old utensils of different shapes and sizes from the cupboard. The heavier the utensil, the more pronounced the sound it will make.

On the rim of the mould, pierce a number of evenly spaced holes, thread some of the line through (in varying lengths) and fix using the nuts and a knot. Make sure your utensils aren't too far from one another, or you will need a gale force wind for them to connect!

Now ask your child to thread along each piece of line as many buttons and beads as he likes. When he's done, tie a knot, making sure that you leave enough room to attach a kitchen utensil to each end. You may need to pierce a hole in the kitchen utensil.

Find a tree with a low hanging branch (so the chime can be reached by little ones) and attach the line rising from the top of the mould to the tree (into which you've already screwed a small hook).

Encourage your child to tap it. Stand back and listen to the pretty music.

Mum might want earmuffs!

You can add these fun items to an outdoor orchestra. This is a great activity for children 2–6.

You will need:

- small recyclable PET plastic bottles with lids or plastic containers
- plain paper to cover the bottles
- sticky tape
- colouring-in pens or pencils
- different objects, such as sand, rice, pasta, water, stones or pebbles, small sticks.

Help your children to cover each of the bottles with paper to disguise the contents, then let them decorate the bottles. Help them fill each bottle with different objects. Head outside, give each child a maraca and then ask them to form a conga line and set off on a maraca march! Whilst you're at it, encourage the children to guess what is in their maraca.

Tin can telephone

Children love having imaginary conversations with anyone and everyone. My daughter used to spend a lot of time talking into her hairbrush and telling me to be quiet while she finished a very important call – don't your own words come back to haunt you! I'm afraid she's now progressed to having a real mobile phone permanently glued to her ear.

However, when she was young, I decided to get on the receiving end of her calls. Together we made a tin can telephone and it became a regular method of communication during our time outside.

You will need:

- two empty soup cans or similar (washed, with no sharp edges)
- paper, sticky tape and colouring-in pens to decorate the outside of the cans
- a screwdriver or other implement to pierce the bottom of the cans
- a long piece of waterproof string.

Cover both cans with paper and ask your child to decorate them. They might like to draw a keypad to make it more realistic.

Carefully pierce a hole in the bottom of each can, pushing from the outside in, so no sharp bits protrude.

Thread the string through the holes and tie a large sturdy knot on the inside of each can. Give one of them to your child, then walk away from one another until the string is taut. Instant communication!

Concepts

Young children are always learning. They will benefit tremendously by witnessing first-hand the amazing lessons Mother Nature can offer. Introducing your children to the concepts of colours, shapes, letters and numbers within the context of nature will provide hours of creative and educational fun.

colours

Colour is everywhere! Grey days, rainbows, autumn/fall leaves, impossibly blue skies, brilliant pink flowers, murky brown mud, an expanse of velvety green lawn. Together, go looking for the colours of nature. Make a collection of items in your child's favourite colour (this is a fun indoor activity too) or simply spend an afternoon hunting for every shade of purple. Photograph your finds, print them out and make a colourful collage when you get home.

RAINBOW COLOUR

The colours of the rainbow are amongst the first that young children will be able to recall. Why not grab a piece of paper and some colouring-in pencils and encourage your child to create their own. When you head back indoors, consider making a simple meal that mimics the colours of the rainbow. Fruit salad is an easy option.

Mixing colour

This is a fun activity that all young children can enjoy. Choose a few objects from your neighbourhood that are secondary or tertiary in colour. For example, a green leaf, purple flower, orange berry, a sweet violet.

Set up a painting area and encourage your child to mix their paints to match the colour of the object. When they feel they are close to the right shade, encourage them to paint a copy of their object.

Whether they manage to match the colour or image, or not is incidental; just letting them explore the concept of colour in this way is fun. The colours of Mother Nature are truly extraordinary and provide the most perfect palette from which children can learn about colour.

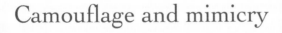

Camouflage and mimicry

Many young children can name up to 10 colours. They are likely to know the three primary colours (red, yellow, blue) followed closely by a range of secondary colours (orange, purple, green, etc.).

What they probably don't think about is the ways colour in nature can be used to hide or mimic. Insects, animals and plants often use camouflage or mimicry as a survival or a reproductive tool. So, next time you and your children are out in the garden, look for green caterpillars cleverly camouflaged on a leaf, a beautiful stick insect clinging to a branch, or a moth or spider resting on the bark of a tree, almost impossible to see.

concepts

PART 5

Cooking by colour

Kids love getting into the kitchen. However, on the whole (and too often), we as parents make the mistake of thinking that 'it's just easier' if adults make and serve the family meals. Adults tend to believe that only they can keep mess to a minimum, that it's quicker, easier and the kids are better off spending time doing something else. Sometimes this can be true, but on the whole there are tremendous benefits to be had by letting our children loose in the kitchen.

The kitchen is alive with concepts and learning mechanisms. Gross and fine motor skills can be refined and improved by encouraging children to undertake basic activities such as pouring, chopping, whisking, grating, etc. Literacy and numeracy skills are improved by the reading of recipes and instructions, along with counting out and measuring ingredients. Self-esteem, creativity, independent thinking, imagination and discovery are also heightened in the kitchen. Plus, it's just plain, good old-fashioned fun.

One of the activities that my children still love is one of their own making. They call it *Cooking by colour*. We tend to do this together once a month or so. Young children will need help and guidance with this, although they can lead the planning process. Children 7+ can not only plan but also take charge of cooking the meals. Here's what you need to do.

Have your children decide on one colour. Now, have them devise a menu (entrée [starter/appetizer], main, dessert) using ingredients that are predominantly only that colour. Below are some sample ideas (many of which you can find on the internet). Be warned, some colours are easier than others!

Red

- Tomato, basil and mozzarella salad
- Panzanella (Tuscan bread salad)
- Meatballs with tomato sauce
- Beetroot risotto or relish
- Red chicken curry
- Eton Mess or Pavlova with red berries (see page **xx** for recipe)
- Trifle with cherries and red jelly
- Strawberry ice cream with pineapple sage flowers

Orange

- Sweet potato gnocchi with burnt sage butter
- Canteloupe/rockmelon and prosciutto
- Pumpkin soup (see page 84)
- Stuffed zucchini/courgette flowers (see page 108)
- Pan-fried salmon with carrot and ginger
- Fresh sliced oranges with honey mascarpone and pistachio biscotti
- Carrot cake

Yellow

- Saffron, prawn and pea risotto (see page 80 for simple pea risotto
- Prawn and mango salad
- Stuffed yellow and red capsicums/bell peppers
- Yellow fish curry
- Smashed bananas with yoghurt and golden syrup
- Lemon sorbet

Green

- Green salad with edible flowers
- Pea and lettuce soup
- Avocado and prawn cocktail
- Guacamole and nachos
- Tuna fillets with Green Goddess sauce (see page 106), green mash and pan-fried zucchinis/courgettes
- Avocado ice cream with pistachios
- Pistachio gelato

Purple blue brown

- Eggplant and haloumi stack
- Blue-eye trevalla with Congo potatoes and steamed greens
- Blueberry zabaglione with borage flowers
- Devils on horseback with baby sausages

Autumn/Fall colour

In autumn/fall, collect a range of different leaves that vary in colour, shape and size.

Once you are back at home, set up an area outside for a painting activity. Ask your children to sticky tape the underside of the leaves they have found to some paper and trace around them. Remove the leaves from the paper and encourage your children to mix their paints until they come close to matching the colour of the leaf they have just removed. Then have them colour in the shape left behind by the leaf.

They might also like to paint a tree (with no leaves), and then attach their real leaves.

let's go nuts!

This is a fun activity suitable for all ages. Buy a selection of nuts in their shells (pistachio and walnuts are ideal). Gently crack the nuts, eat the contents and then encourage your children to paint the discarded shells. They can create insect creatures, simple pretty patterns or funny faces. If you have a drill, you can make a small hole in each shell and your children can then thread them onto some stretchy fishing wire (cotton or string will also do) to make funky necklaces and bracelets.

concepts

shapes

Squiggly, oval, rectangular, square, wrinkly, triangular, perfect circle or heart shaped. Your child can find them all outside in varying sizes and she'll probably invent a few more of her own.

Bubble play

Whizzing about on the breeze, bubbles are a visual delight, while the gloopy bubble mix affords a lovely tactile experience. If possible, choose a day with a slight breeze for this simple activity.

Using store-bought or homemade bubble liquid (two parts dishwashing liquid, one part water and a few drops of glycerine), find a place where the bubbles are likely to catch the breeze. Encourage your child to blow upward and then count the bubbles as they spiral away.

Finding love

Head outside with a camera and your child's journal and spend some time hunting for heart-shaped objects. They are easier to find than you might think. Take photos of each of them (or collect them if you can). When you return home, your child can print them out and make a heart-warming (pun intended) collage in his journal of all that he has found.

Leaf faces

This is fun to do! From their leaf collection, your children choose leaves of different shapes and sizes and arrange them on a piece of paper to make a shape. They might make a leaf person or face, a boat, a house or an animal. Have your children sticky tape the leaves lightly to the paper and trace around them, then remove the leaves and gently and colour in the space left behind with a design of their choice. Or they could make an entire person if they wished.

concepts

Buy a Wollemi

One of the quirkiest leaf arrangements to have been found is on a truly remarkable plant discovered in Australia in 1994 by a bushwalker named David Noble. Nicknamed the Dinosaur Pine, it is believed to have flourished in Australia over 200 million years ago when dinosaurs were roaming the earth.

It was thought to be extinct until David found a tiny stand of trees in a remote canyon outside Sydney. Cuttings of the trees were taken and have been propagated so successfully that botanists believe there is no danger of this tree disappearing again. Very hardy, the Wollemi pine, as it is now called, does really well indoors in a pot, which is great because they help fight indoor pollution. The Wollemi pine is one of the most effective and efficient plants for detoxing indoor environments. So if you have one inside, it will be like a super set of lungs, breathing in all the bad stuff floating in the air and giving you back sweet, clean air in return. The tree will eventually grow too large to be inside, but at that time it can be planted out in the garden.

AMAZING LEAVES

Did you know that there is a water lily leaf big enough to hold the weight of a small child? And another plant with leaves so large that it's common name is Elephant Ears? Others are tiny and delicate, some thick and fleshy, some are heart-shaped and still others don't look like leaves at all. Mother Nature provides literally hundreds of leaf shapes, types and sizes.

With a cry of 'We're going on a leaf hunt!', set off on an exploration with your child and find as many as you can – you'll be amazed at how many you come across. When you are back from your adventure, your child can stick them into their nature journal.

Children 7 + might like to research exactly how many leaf shapes there are and whether particular leaf shapes are peculiar to certain families of plants, and then create a diagram showing the main shapes and sizes. They could also collect some and press them to make an interesting artwork.

Precious crystals

Rocks, stones and pebbles are favourites in our home. At last count, my daughter had around 150, which she has amassed over the years and classified by shape.

Collection points have included footpaths, parks, nature strips, the beach, a vacant building site, a friend's farm, the gutter, car parks and people's driveways. She is quite the bowerbird and has developed a keen eye for unusually shaped stones. And while she is now a teen, she still refers to them as 'crystals' and sorts through them regularly. When she was little, she would carry them about in her purse or doll's pram and, inevitably, many would end up in my handbag. Every now and then I continue to supplement her collection by adding a few real crystals or brightly coloured smooth glass. If you have regular access to a beach, you could encourage your children to collect shells instead and start their own collection.

letters and numbers

'1, 2, skip a few, 99, 100'. Assisting your child with foundation skills, such as literacy and numeracy, is important – but it doesn't have to be hard. Use the outdoors as a handy resource, and help them count a cluster of berries on a shrub or the number of cars that pass by your house. Encourage them to shout out the house numbers as you walk around your suburb. How many bird calls can they hear? How many 'hands' can they see on a maple tree?

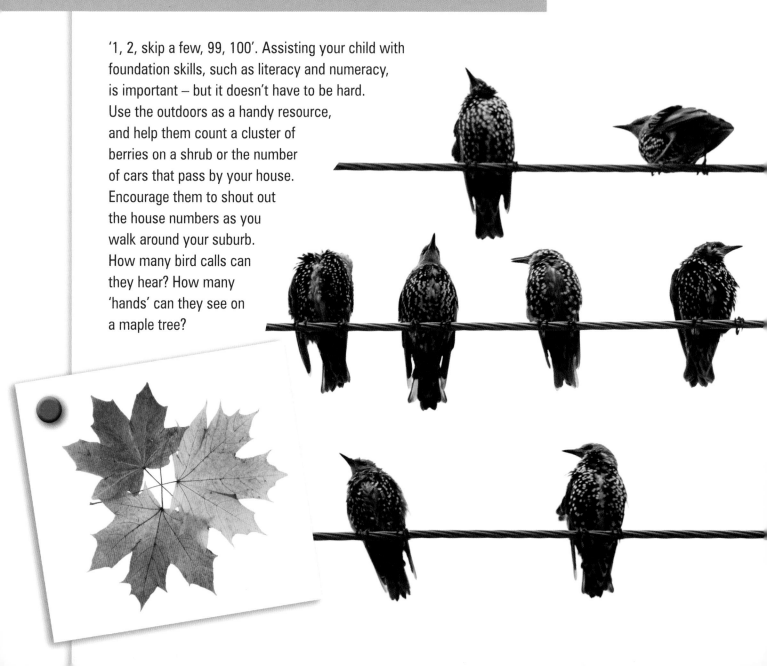

Writing it down

This is an activity suited to both young children who are just starting to write simple words and older children who are becoming more proficient with writing short little stories. For children aged 3–6, choose one word relating to a room in your home and ask them to try writing it down on a piece of paper. They can also do a drawing to accompany the word. You can do this for each room in your home if you wish. For children 7+, encourage them to make up a short story using that word complete with illustrations. Not only does this activity assist with literacy, it is also sure to fire imaginations!

Counting cows

Next time you and your children take a trip to the country, encourage them to count cows. Less likely to send them to sleep than counting sheep ☺, cows are big and easy for little eyes to keep track of in a paddock or stockyard. See how many calves they can spot, how many black cows there are as opposed to cows with markings, and so on.

If walking through a paddock/field with cows, you might also encourage them to count and jump over the cowpats they come across — they are irresistible to most young children. And if you have a sturdy plastic bag to hand, you can take dried pats home to use as fertiliser on your garden. They also make great footballs when playing in the paddocks. Just make sure they are completely dry!

concepts

DIY board game

Think of this game as a Stone Age version of a modern-day board game – it's just so much fun to create and a great rainy day activity. Although it is relatively time-consuming and probably best suited to older children, it is a great project to encourage concentration and literacy and numeracy skills.

You will need:

- found objects such as gumnuts, berries, pebbles or shells that can be used as pieces to move around the game
- permanent markers
- piece of strong flat cardboard, 45 cm square
- ruler
- colouring-in pens, fine markers and fluorescent pens
- 1 die.

Together, collect some objects on which your children can draw a figure of some kind, so that each one takes on a different look or choose objects that are completely different to one another.

Now, have them make up a game and transcribe it onto the piece of cardboard. It might be inspired by Snakes and Ladders or a treasure hunt, or a simple numbered board game. Themes could include reaching the end of a rainbow, following a trail to find treasure, a bushland adventure (over mountains, through rivers, avoiding snakes, etc.). The scope of the game is limited only by your children's imagination.

Daisy chains

Dandelions and Capeweed are perfect for this fun, pretty activity, but any flower with a long, fleshy, thick stem will do, such as lavender or daisies.

Encourage your child to pick as many as they can find with as long a stem as possible – counting as they go. Once they think they have enough, use your fingernail to make a small slit at the end of the stem. Then help your child poke the stem of another flower into the slit and gently pull it through until the flower is fixed in place. Continue doing this until you reach the desired length.

You can make garlands, crowns, necklaces, anklets and bracelets. My daughter, now a teenager still makes daisy chains over the summer months. If you have a very young child, simply sprinkling the flowers in their hair is just as much fun.

time

Tick, tock, goes the clock ... sometimes too fast for adults and often way too slowly for children! Don't worry too much about teaching young children to tell the time; that will come later. Instead, consider letting Mother Nature provide some fun messages on the concept.

For young children, time is obscure and virtually indefinable. It's like a form of magic. They have little concept of the difference between a minute, half an hour, a day, a week. Certainly for little ones, understanding the difference between a month and a year is impossible.

Children mark time by events in their life (as do most adults), such as when Mummy goes to work, when she comes back, when they are hungry, when the sun comes up and when it goes down. However, they are not truly understanding time, rather observing events that take place regularly one after the other.

A birthday might be much anticipated, but the time taken getting to that magical day is just a blur of other events until you tell them that today is their 'big day'.

Forget trying to explain the finer points of daylight saving to a three year old or exactly how long it's going to take to get there on a road trip. Instead, celebrate their perception of time. In a world of stress and rushing here and there, whenever possible, a young child shouldn't have to worry about time passing. As long as there is time to play, sleep and eat, at this stage of their lives they will benefit tremendously from having big slabs of it to daydream and observe at their own speed.

concepts

Time capsule

Time capsules can be on a grand public scale or a small private offering. Why not encourage your children to devise their own? This activity is probably better suited to children five or older, but littler ones will also love helping to select items. Be guided by your child's ability.

Let your children set the period of time that the capsule will be buried in the garden – try and encourage at least six months to a year, if not more. (For little children that will most likely prove impossible.) Together, write a short story about them at the time they have nominated: their family and things that are happening in their life (their favourite toy, food, pet, TV show, etc.). You might want to encourage them to include some ideas or drawings of what they think they will be doing when it's time to dig up the capsule.

Have your children include some memorabilia: a photocopied page from their favourite book, a special treasure, the newspaper of the day, anything they wish to include. An old chamois container makes a great capsule. You might like to use a calendar to mark off the days until 'dig up day'.

With preschoolers about to start school, aim to bury the time capsule just before they start, and then dig it up when their first year of school is coming to an end. It is likely that the differences in them, their likes and dislikes are much more pronounced as starting school heralds a big period of change.

The world as a ball and time on the other side

This is a simple activity to undertake if you are struggling to explain why the sun goes up and down (along with the moon) and why friends on the other side of the world are sleeping while you are wide awake. Children under six may struggle with this concept, so be guided by your child's ability.

First, explain to your child that the earth is like an enormous ball that sits next to, spins around and then in turn also whizzes around another huge, bright ball called the sun. Blow up a balloon and draw a rough approximation of the continents on it, then hang it from something so you can move a torch around it.

In a darkened room, using the torch as the sun, shine it brightly on your country. Encourage your child to look at their friend's country on the other side. Hey presto: night time on one side, sunshine on the other!

Up she grows!

While trees never appear to grow before our eyes, our children do. By measuring the growth of both, children gain a greater understanding of how quickly they and their environment grow and change.

Visit a garden centre and buy a tree that is at least a head taller than your child. It should be a relatively fast-growing species with smooth bark, such as a Chinese tallow tree, crepe myrtle or crabapple – which will also eventually double as a brilliant climbing tree for young children. All have good autumn/fall colour too. Find a spot in your garden and plant it.

If you don't have space for a new tree, adopt a young tree on a nature strip, in a park or other open area to which you have regular access. Many councils have tree-planting programs, in which they encourage people to participate.

Using a texta or ribbon, measure and mark your child's height on the tree. Measure the tree as well. Revisit your tree each month and record both its progress and the progress of your child. Given the tree will grow, taking your child's measurement with it up the trunk, you'll need to undertake a little calculation if you wish to get an accurate idea of how she/he has grown. You could place a long timber stake by the tree and mark it in line with the measurement you make on the tree. By the time the tree is too high to measure accurately, your child will probably have lost interest in this project – which is a blessing unless you like scaling ladders and somewhat complicated mathematics!

PART 5

concepts

web of life

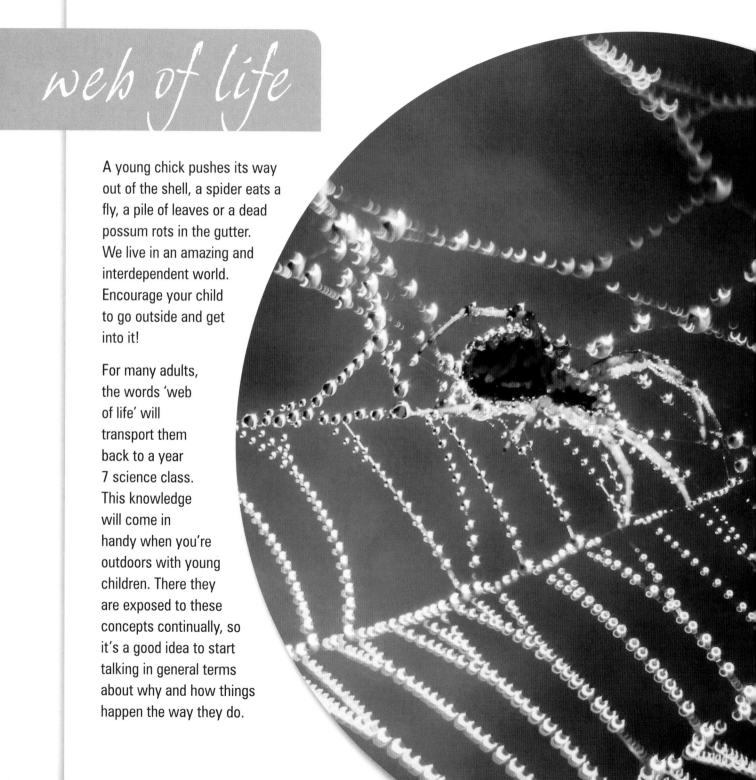

A young chick pushes its way out of the shell, a spider eats a fly, a pile of leaves or a dead possum rots in the gutter. We live in an amazing and interdependent world. Encourage your child to go outside and get into it!

For many adults, the words 'web of life' will transport them back to a year 7 science class. This knowledge will come in handy when you're outdoors with young children. There they are exposed to these concepts continually, so it's a good idea to start talking in general terms about why and how things happen the way they do.

Spider watching

Everything in nature is interdependent. We are all part of one enormous web and either directly or indirectly rely on each other for survival. Talk in simple, positive terms about the web of life.

For example, find a spider in a web, sit down with your child and observe it. If they want to squash the spider, remind them that spiders eat the annoying flies that buzz around our heads on a summer's day and that very soon something may well eat the spider. Everything has its place. Observing chickens scratching for insects and seeds is another good example. Chat about how the chicken eats insects, keeping them away from our veggie patch, and how they help disperse seeds (in their poo or just by scratching around). Then, when used as a fertiliser, their poo also helps the plants we eat to grow and in turn nourish us. Round and round it goes.

Nature's Cupcakes

For this activity, use our Simplicity Chocolate Cake recipe on page 21, but instead put the batter into cupcake tins rather than a single cake tin and bake for a little less time, probably no more than 10–15 minutes.

Encourage your children to make the cupcakes and then decorate them to look like spiders, ladybirds, caterpillars, dragonflies, or other sweet little insects from nature. They could also make little nature babies. Essentially, your child can pick their favourite insect and then decorate away. They can make some basic butter icing (coloured with the food dye of their choice), and use items such as licorice canes, Smarties, sprinkles, Freckles, jubes, jellies and jellybeans to create their masterpieces. Fondant can also be used if you want a challenge.

If you observe/celebrate Halloween, consider doing this activity at that time and sharing the goodies with your neighbours.

concepts

PART 5

Death and decay

Once you are outside, examples of life and death, or the cycle of life, will invariably present themselves. When you feel your children are old enough, you might encourage them to observe the process of decay on a dead lamb, possum or other poor hapless creature. Older children can be morbidly fascinated by dead animals.

Watching annual plants shoot, grow and die is also a good way for children to understand the cycle of life. Buy a young annual plant (marigold, climbing bean or sunflower are good options) and have them plant it where they will have ready access to it. Children 7+ can then be encouraged to regularly record its growth, flowering, fruiting or seeding, and eventual death. They can do this by making sketches or taking photographs to include in a journal, or by creating a diagram.

The miracle of birth

Young children are fascinated by the process of birth, and may ask you endlessly about where they came from and how they got out of Mummy's tummy. When the time is right, use simple and positive language to describe this process to them. Consider a visit to a farm or zoo during spring, when many animals are being born, and let them experience the miracle of birth first-hand.

My daughter, now 14, once had the opportunity to help me deliver a lamb at our farm. It was very early in the morning, drizzling and freezing cold. Worse, we were still in our pyjamas. But ask her to name a moment when she was filled with wonder and love and she will always mention this as an incredibly special experience. I must admit that she did become a vegetarian for some time afterwards, but her love of pan-fried lamb chops with mash and greens eventually overtook her desire to save the lambs of the world!

You might also want to consider renting an incubator containing fertilised chicken's eggs and hatching your own chicks at home. Some companies supply kits that are ready to go and they will come and collect the chicks once hatching has occurred.

Glossary

Words and names

AUSTRALIA/NEW ZEALAND	UNITED STATES/CANADA	UNITED KINGDOM
Autumn	Fall	Autumn
Band-Aid®	Band-Aid®	Plaster, sticking plaster
Beetroot	Beets	Beetroot
Biscuits	Cookies	Biscuits
Broad beans	Fava beans	Broad beans
Bush	Forest	Forest
Canteloupe/rockmelon	Canteloupe	Canteloupe
Capsicum	Bell pepper	Pepper or sweet pepper
Caster sugar	Superfine sugar	Caster sugar
Chickpeas	Chickpeas or Garbanzo beans	Chickpeas
Chillies	Chilli peppers	Chillies
Cordial	Squash	Cordial
Coriander	Cilantro	Coriander
Cornflour	Cornstarch	Cornflour
Damper	Australian damper	Australian damper
Dandelion heads	Blowballs or dandelion clocks	Dandelion clocks
Eggplant	Eggplant	Aubergine
Entrée	Appetiser	Entrée
Fish Fingers	Fish Sticks	Fish Fingers
Flat leaf parsley/ continental parsley	Flat leaf parsley	Continental parsley
Full cream milk	Whole milk or 3% milk	Full fat milk
Icing sugar	Confectioner's sugar	Icing sugar
Local Council	Local Authority	Local Authority
Lolly	Candy	Lolly/boiled sweet
Main course	Entrée	Main course
Marigold/ tagetes	Marigold/tagetes	Marigold
Paprika	Paprika/pimento	Sweet paprika

AUSTRALIA/NEW ZEALAND	UNITED STATES/CANADA	UNITED KINGDOM
Permanent marker	Sharpie	Permanent marker
Pikelet	Flat crumpet	Pikelet
Plain flour	All-purpose flour	Plain flour
Pumpkin	Pumpkin	Pumpkin
Rocket	Arugula	Rocket
Rubber band	Rubber band	Rubber band/elastic band
Scone	Biscuit	Scone
Self-raising flour	Self-raising flour	Self-raising flour
Serviettes/napkins	Napkins	Serviettes/napkins
Silverbeet	Chard	Silverbeet/chard
Skim milk	Skim or skimmed milk	Skimmed milk
Snow peas	Snow peas/sugar peas	Mangetout
Sour cream/crème fraîche	Sour cream	Sour cream/crème fraîche
Shallot	Green onion/scallion	Spring onion
Squash/marrow	Squash	Vegetable marrow
Sticky tape	Sticky tape	Sello tape
Stockings/pantyhose	Pantyhose	Stockings/pantyhose
Sweet potato	Sweet potato/yam	Sweet potato
Sweet corn	Corn	Sweet corn
Tahini	Sesame paste/tahini	Tahini/tahini
Tasty/cheddar cheese	Cheddar cheese	Tasty/cheddar cheese
Tissues/facial tissues	Kleenex	Tissues
Tomato sauce	Ketchup	Ketchup/tomato sauce/red sauce
Yabby	Crayfish	Crayfish
Zucchini	Zucchini	Courgette

Seasons

SOUTHERN HEMISPHERE
Spring – September/October/November
Summer – December/January/February
Autumn – March/April/May
Winter – June/July/August

NORTHERN HEMISPHERE
Spring – March/April/May
Summer – June/July/August
Fall – September/October/November
Winter – December/January/February

Conversion charts

LIQUID AND VOLUME

Cup and spoon size	Metric	Imperial
1/4 tsp		1.2 ml
1/2 tsp		2.5 ml
1 tsp		5.0 ml
1/2 tbsp (1 1/2 tsp)		7.5 ml
1 tbsp (3 tsp)	1/2 fl oz	15 ml
1/8 cup	1 fl oz	30 ml
1/4 cup (4 tbsp)	2 fl oz	60 ml
1/3 cup (5 tbsp)	3 fl oz	80 ml
1/2 cup (8 tbsp)	4 fl oz	120 ml
2/3 cup (10 tbsp)	5 fl oz	160 ml
3/4 cup (12 tbsp)	6 fl oz	180 ml
1 cup (16 tbsp)	8 fl oz (1/2 pint)	250 ml
1 1/4 cups	10 fl oz	300 ml
1 1/2 cups	12 fl oz	350 ml
2 cups	16 fl oz	475 ml
2 1/2 cups	20 fl oz	625 ml
3 cups	24 fl oz (1 1/2 pint)	700 ml
4 cups	32 fl oz (1 quart)	950 ml
4 quarts	128 fl oz (1 gallon)	3.8 L

WEIGHT

Imperial	Metric	Imperial	Metric
1/4 oz	7 g	9 oz	255 g
1/2 oz	15 g	10 oz (2/3 lb)	300 g
1 oz	30 g	11 oz	310 g
2 oz	55 g	12 oz (3/4 lb)	340 g
3 oz	85 g	13 oz	370 g
4 oz (1/4 lb)	115 g	14 oz	400 g
5 oz (1/3 lb)	140 g	15 oz	425 g
6 oz	170 g	16 oz (1 lb)	450 g
7 oz	200 g	2 pounds	900 g
8 oz (1/2 lb)	225 g		

BAKING PAN SIZES

	US	Volume	Metric	Volume
Rectangular	11 x 7 x 2 inches	6 cups	28 x 18 x 5 cm	1.4 litres
	13 x 9 x 2 inches	4 cups	33 x 23 x 5 cm	3.3 litres
Round	8 x 2 inches	6 cups	20 x 5 cm	1.4 litres
	9 x 2 inches	8 cups	23 x 5cm	1.9 litres
	10 x 2 inches	10 cups	25 x 5 cm	2.6 litres
Square	8 x 8 x 2 inches	8 cups	20 x 20 x 5 cm	1.9 litres
	9 x 9 x 2 inches	10 cups	23 x 23 x 5 cm	2.4 litres
	10 x 10 x 2 inches	12 cups	25 x 25 x 5 cm	2.8 litres
Loaf	8 x 3 x 2 1/2 inches	4 cups	20 x 10 x 6 cm	948 ml
	9 x 5 x 3 inches	8 cups	23 x 13 x 8 cm	1.9 litres

TEMPERATURE

°C Electric	°C Fan-forced	°F	Gas
120	100	250	1
150	130	300	2
160	140	325	3
180	160	350	4
190	170	375	5
200	180	400	6
230	210	450	7
250	230	500	8